L'INSTANT
CHANEL

www.chanel.com

L'INSTANT
CHANEL

L'INSTANT
CHANEL

Adrian, the amateur botanist, could never part with his Toby or Charles. Charles is designed by Antonio Citterio. www.bebitalia.com

B&B Italia Stores: London, SW3 2AS - 250 Brompton Road - Tel. 020 7591 8111
New York, 150 East 58th Street - 138 Greene Street, SoHo - Tel. 1 800 872 1697 - info@bbitaliausa.com
Milano, via Durini, 14 Tel. 02 76 44 41 - **Paris,** 35, Rue du Bac Tel. 01 55 35 14 35
München, Maximiliansplatz 21 - Tel. 089 461 368 0 - **Berlin,** Torstrasse 140 - Tel. +49 3024 04 77 377
Wien, Spätauf GmbH A -1010 Wien Parkring 20 - F DW 40 T. +43 (0) 1-512 22 30 info@bebitalia-wien.at

DESIGN PORTRAIT.

THE ALL-NEW BMW i8.
A CARBON REVOLUTION.

The new BMW i8 embodies the future of sports cars – with a progressive design made from super-light, super-strong carbon fibre, breathtaking driving performance and maximum efficiency. Thanks to its innovative BMW eDrive technology, the new BMW i8 combines an electric drive with a BMW TwinPower Turbo combustion engine that achieves a power output of 266 kW (362 hp) and can accelerate from 0–100 km/h in 4.4 seconds. And all this with a fuel consumption of 2.1 litres per 100 km on the EU test cycle. The new BMW i8 is the most impressive proof to date that efficiency doesn't mean having to do without passion. Find out more at bmw-i.com/i8

BMW i. BORN ELECTRIC.

BMW EfficientDynamics

| BMW i8 | 49 g CO_2/km | 266 kW (362 hp) |

Official fuel economy figures for the BMW i8: Weighted combined cycle: mpg 134.5 (2.1 l/100 km), CO_2 emissions 49 g/km, power output (engine) 170/231 kW/hp, power output (electric motor) 96/131 kW/hp, total average energy consumption per 62 miles/100 km (weighted combined cycle) 11.9 kWh, customer-orientated total range up to 373 miles. Maximum electric range value 23 miles, common average electric range value (e-Drive only) up to 23 miles. The BMW i8 is a plug-in hybrid electric vehicle that requires electricity for charging. Range figures may vary depending on different factors, including but not limited to individual driving style, climatic conditions, route characteristics and preconditioning. New BMW i vehicles are available at authorised BMW i Agents.

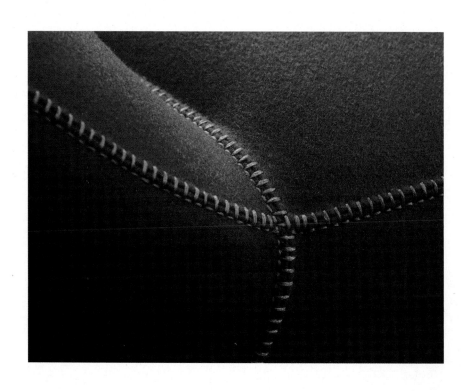

MITT

DESIGNED BY
CLAUDIA + HARRY WASHINGTON

JULY

➜
ARCHITECT FABIO
NOVEMBRE POWER NAPS
AT THE NEW AC MILAN
HQ. HE'S IN THE VAULT
WHERE THE UEFA
CHAMPIONS LEAGUE CUP,
WHICH THE TEAM LAST
WON IN 2007, IS KEPT,
ALONG WITH FRANCO
BARESI'S FINAL SHIRT,
FROM 1997. SEE PAGE 054

JULY

↑
THE SOARING GLASS DOME OF THE NEW JÉRÔME
SEYDOUX-PATHÉ FOUNDATION HQ IN PARIS, SEE PAGE 080

BISAZZA

MOSAICO

LONDON, 60 SLOANE AVENUE
www.bisazza.com

ERASED
HERITAGE

BOCHUM | COLOGNE | STUTTGART | HAMBURG | MUNICH
BERLIN | ZURICH | VIENNA | LONDON | MOSCOW | NEW YORK
WWW.JAN-KATH.COM

JAN
KATH

Wallpaper*

f Wallpaper.com

twitter.com/wallpapermag

World Headquarters

Blue Fin Building,
110 Southwark Street,
London SE1 0SU,
United Kingdom
Tel: 44.20 3148 5000
Fax: 44.20 3148 8119
E-mail: contact@wallpaper.com

Subscriptions

Tel: 44.845 676 7778
Fax: 44.1444 445 599
E-mail: ipcsubs@qss-uk.com
Order online at:
www.wallpaper.com

Editorial

Editor-in-Chief
Tony Chambers

Editorial Director
Richard Cook

Senior Contributing Editor
Nick Compton

Managing Editor
Oliver Adamson

Editors-at-Large
Leïla Latchin,
Emma O'Kelly,
Henrietta Thompson,
Suzanne Trocmé

Art

Creative Director
Sarah Douglas

Art Director
Lee Belcher

Senior Designer
Aneel Kalsi

Designer
Ben McLaughlin

iPad Designer
Sine Ringgaard Jørgensen

Intern
Melanie Dagher

Photography

Photography Director
James Reid

Associate Photography Editor
Kate Barrett

Interns
Ryan Grimley, Rachel Lamb

Architecture / Design

Architecture Editor
Ellie Stathaki

Design Editor
Rosa Bertoli

Interns
Catarina de Almeida Brito,
Leigh Theodore Vlassis

Interiors / Entertaining

Interiors Director
Benjamin Kempton

Interiors Editor
Amy Heffernan

Entertaining Director
Melina Keays

Interiors Assistant
Maria Sobrino

Interiors Coordinator
Sujata Burman

Interns
Camille Boyer, Emily Moloney

Beauty / Lifestyle

Beauty & Lifestyle Director
Emma Moore

Intern
Elizabeth Hutton

Travel

Travel Editor
Lauren Ho

Intern
Athena Fierou

Fashion

Fashion Director
Isabelle Kountoure

Fashion Editor
Mathew Stevenson-Wright

Junior Fashion Editor
Zoë Sinclair

Fashion Coordinator
Alice Shaughnessy

Bookings Editor
Minna Vauhkonen

Watches & Jewellery Director
Caragh McKay

Jewellery Editor-at-Large
Franceline Prat

Interns
Pierre Crolard, Sarah Starkey,
Julia Vojtovic

Production

Chief Sub Editor
Bridget Downing

Production Editor
Anne Soward

Acting Sub Editor
Maksymilian Fus Mickiewicz

Sub Editor
Léa Teuscher

iPad Production Manager
Leonard Burns

iPad Production Coordinator
Daniel Short

Wallpaper.com

Online Editor
Malaika Byng

Acting Online Fashion Editor
Katrina Israel

Online Fashion Editor
Apphia Michael

Online Assistant Editor
Jessica Klingelfuss

Designer
Ben Ewing

Junior Designers
Michael Ainscough,
James Davies

Web Developer
Marcin Stepniewski

Editorial Business Assistant
David Paw

**Office Manager and
PA to Tony Chambers**
TF Chan

Contributing editors

Design
Albert Hill

Media
Stephen Armstrong

Production
Sara Norrman

Typography
Paul Barnes

International editors

US Editor
Michael Reynolds

New York Editor
Pei-Ru Keh

Italy Editor-at-Large
J J Martin

Japan Editor
Jens H Jensen

Brazil Editor-at-Large
Scott Mitchem

Germany Editor-at-Large
Sophie Lovell

Hamburg Editor
Ina Becker

Australia Editor
Carrie Hutchinson

Mexico and Central America Editor
Pablo León de la Barra

Buenos Aires Editor
Mariana Rapoport

Middle East Editor
Warren Singh-Bartlett

Singapore Editor
Daven Wu

Publishing & Marketing

Publishing Director
Gord Ray

Publisher
Kirsty Mulhern

Advertising

Commercial Director
Paula Cain
Tel: 44.20 3148 7724

**Fashion, Watches
& Jewellery Manager**
Anu Pai
Tel: 44.20 3148 7764

Sales Manager
Ben Duggan
Tel: 44.20 3148 7722

Advertising Business Manager
Amanda Asigno

Finance Advertising Coordinator
Barron Nouban

Intern
Margot Dallier

Production Controller
Nick Percival

Marketing

Marketing Manager
Caroline Sampson

Wallpaper.com

Senior Digital Sales Manager
Ryan Green
Tel: 44.20 3148 7726

Digital Project Manager
Claudia Mastromauro

Wallpaper* Bespoke

Bespoke Director
Rebecca Morris
Tel: 44.20 3148 7726

Editor
Simon Mills

Art Director
Ben Jarvis

Account Manager
Matthew Johnston
Tel: 44.20 3148 7704

Designer
Luke Fenech

Bespoke Coordinator
Fred Jezeph

Art Intern
Queenie Wong

Special Projects & Events

Head of Special Projects
Thomas Aastad

Advertising offices

International Sales Director
Malcolm Young
Tel: 44.20 3148 7718

USA
**Advertising Manager
(Northeast)**
Ilaria Anghinoni
Tel: 1.646 389 5554

**Advertising Manager
(Southeast)**
Ana Torres de Navarra
Tel: 1.305 662 4754

**International Sales Director
(West Coast)**
Malcolm Young
Tel: 44.20 3148 7718

ITALY
Advertising Manager
Paolo Cesana

Design Executives
Rosalba Basile, Marcella Biggi

Fashion Executive
Cristiana Catizone
Tel: 39.02 844 0441
Fax: 39.02 848 10287

GERMANY, AUSTRIA
AND SWITZERLAND
Advertising Manager
Peter Wolfram
Tel: 49.89 9924 93990
Fax: 49.89 9924 93999

CHINA
Advertising Manager
Maggie Li
Tel: 86.10 6588 0051

BRAZIL
Advertising Manager
Paolo Mongeri
Tel: 55.21 98393 9495

FRANCE
Advertising Manager
Magali Riboud
Tel: 33.1 42 56 33 36

HONG KONG, TAIWAN,
AND KOREA
Advertising Manager
Herb Moskowitz
Tel: 852.2838 8702
Fax: 852.2572 5468

JAPAN, MALAYSIA
AND SINGAPORE
Advertising Manager
Julie Harrison
Tel: 65.6463 3220
Fax: 65.6469 6282

INDIA
Advertising Manager
Ravi Lalwani
Tel: 91.22 4220 2118

Circulation / Subscriptions

Deputy Circulation Manager
Gemma Melhuish

**Senior International
Circulation Executive**
Richard Wilkinson

**Senior Subscriptions
Marketing Manager**
Nikki Phillips

Finance

Deputy Management Accountant
Mark Adams

Corporate

Managing Director, Southbank
Jackie Newcombe

Corporate Public Relations
Victoria Higham

Production Manager
John Botten

Assistant Syndication Manager
Efi Mandrides

Wallpaper*, ISSN 1364-4475, is published monthly, 12 times a year, by The Wallpaper* Group, a division of IPC Media Ltd. © 2014 Wallpaper* IPC Media Ltd. US agent: Mercury International, 365 Blair Road, Avenel, NJ 07001. Periodicals paid at Rahway, NJ. POSTMASTER: Send address changes to Wallpaper*, 365 Blair Road, Avenel, NJ 07001.
Reproduction in whole or in part without written permission is strictly prohibited. All prices and credits are accurate at time of going to press but are subject to change. Manuscripts, photos, drawings and other materials submitted must be accompanied by a stamped, self-addressed envelope. Wallpaper* cannot be held responsible for any unsolicited material. Subscription rate for Wallpaper* for one year (12 issues) is UK £64, USA $135, Europe €127, rest of the world £132.
For subscriptions contact: (in the UK/ROW) IPC Media Ltd, PO Box 272, Haywards Heath, West Sussex, RH16 3FS, tel: 44.844 848 0848, e-mail: ipcsubs@quadrantsubs.com; (in the USA) IPC Media Ltd, PO Box 4661, Chesterfield, MO 63006-9966, tel: 1.888 313 5528, email: ipccustomerservice@quadrantsubs.com (USA). Repro by Rhapsody. Printed by Southernprint Ltd and Wyndeham Grange. Distributed by Marketforce (UK) Ltd, 4th Floor, Blue Fin Building, 110 Southwark Street, London SE1 0SU, tel: 44.20 3148 3555

She's a fan.

MANDARIN ORIENTAL
THE HOTEL GROUP

OUR DESIGN AWARD #63

design by LINDBERG · made by LINDBERG

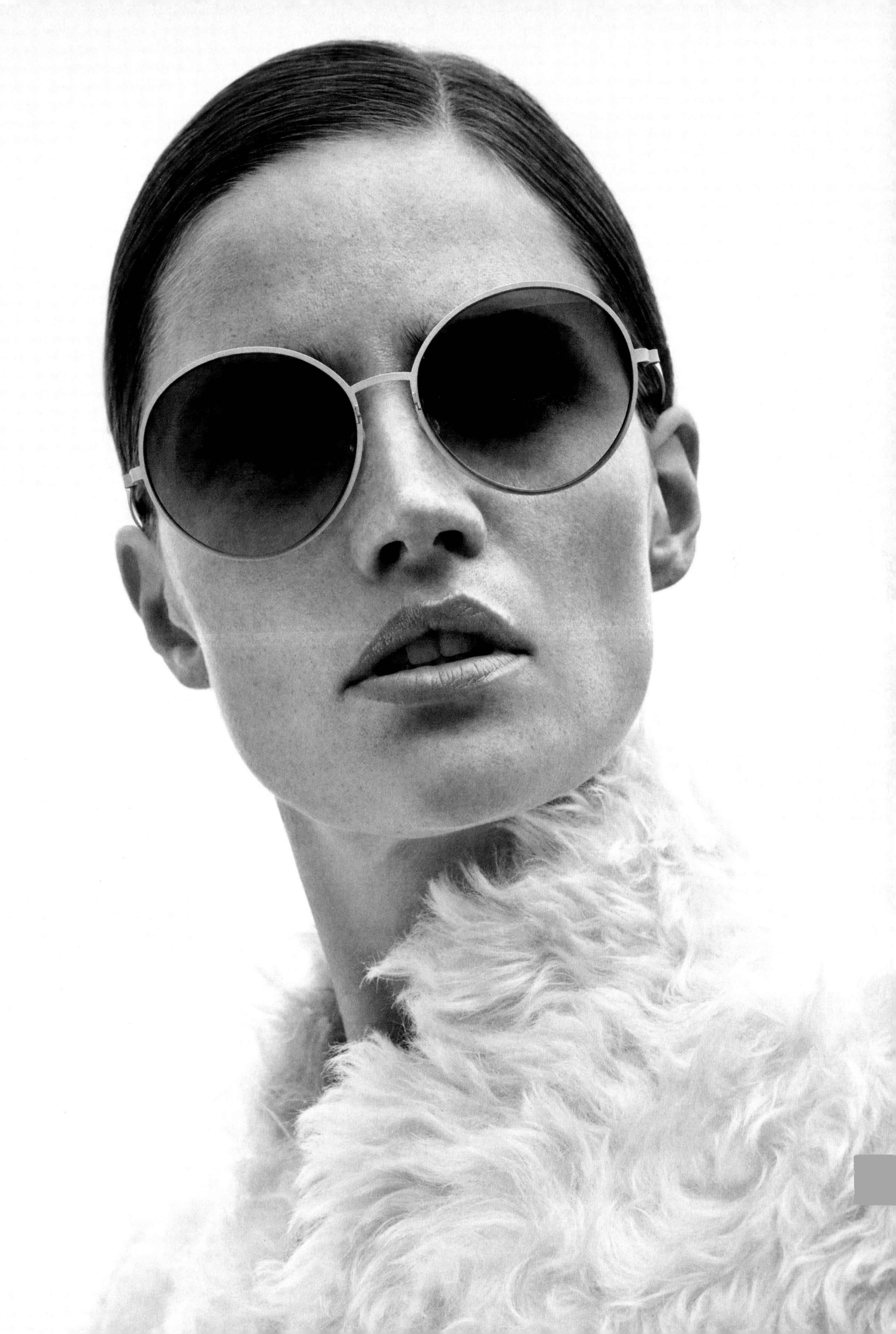

LINDBERG 8584

CONTRIBUTORS

PHILIPPE PARRENO ∧
Artist

This month's back page recipe (page 226) is a challenging little number – a key ingredient is spleen – by French artist Philippe Parreno (W*176). Parreno doesn't create series of objects but, rather, employs film, sculpture, performance, drawing and text to make the overall exhibition his 'object'. One of his best-known pieces, made with Douglas Gordon, is *Zidane: A 21st Century Portrait*, in which the Real Madrid player's every move was followed during a match by 17 cameras.

JENS H JENSEN ∧
Japan Editor

Wallpaper's new Japan Editor has written a profile of the Japanese furniture maker Maruni (page 091). After studying Japanese at SOAS in London, Jensen moved to Japan in 2002. Having worked for a small Dutch architecture practice and Japanese branding consultancy, he turned to writing and other projects this year – his plan being to tell the world about the best of Japan. 'Maruni is important because it combines Japanese craftsmanship and attention to detail with super hi-tech production robots,' he says.

RENZO PIANO ∨
Architect

Italian architect Renzo Piano is behind this month's limited-edition cover, a drawing of his new HQ for the Jérôme Seydoux-Pathé Foundation in Paris. The organically shaped building proved an inspiring space to gather and photograph the world's best emerging architects for our Architects Directory 2014 (page 080). Piano's practice is responsible for some of the world's most eye-catching landmarks – including The New York Times Building in Manhattan and The Shard in London. He won the Pritzker Prize in 1998.

RICHARD KOLKER ∨
Artist

Richard Kolker is one of the world's leading CG photographic artists. He's taught at the Slade School of Fine Art, UCL, and his work resides in several international museum collections. For Wallpaper* he interpreted the designs of the practices in our Architects Directory (page 080). 'Instead of just creating visualisations of the work from architects' plans and photographs, I wanted to create a series of simulated still lifes of the buildings in model form,' he explains.

LEONARDO SCOTTI ∧
Photographer

Leonardo Scotti is a freelance photographer and artist based in Milan. He works with Pierpaolo Ferrari and Maurizio Cattelan on projects such as their magazine *ToiletPaper*, for fashion brands including Missoni and Roberto Cavalli, and undertakes fine art and street photography projects. For this issue, he photographed the still-life pages for The W* House (from page 099). 'It was interesting to play with combinations of furniture to create simple shapes,' he says.

LEANDRO FARINA ∧
Photographer

Leandro Farina is a London-based photographer who took on this month's Space story (page 214). Farina, who has recently been working for *Vogue* Japan, Dunhill and British Airways, styled the shoot with the feel of a deserted furniture factory. 'It was loosely based around forgotten spaces and de-industrialisation,' says Farina. He's a regular contributor here at Wallpaper*, with a sophisticated and graphic style that makes his still-life work bold and rather glamorous.

ILLUSTRATOR: MAGDA ANTONIUK WRITER: PAUL MCCANN

ERIC WHITACRE · GLOBAL CITIZEN + GRAMMY® AWARD-WINNING COMPOSER

NEW TUMI FLAGSHIP | 211 REGENT STREET, LONDON, W1B 4NF
170 PICCADILLY, MAYFAIR, LONDON, W1J 9EJ
265 CANARY WHARF SHOPPING CENTRE, CABOT SQ., LONDON, E14 4QT

TUMI.COM

RH

RESTORATION HARDWARE

THE BEN SOLEIMANI
RUG COLLECTION

BEN SOLEIMANI, DESIGNER/COLLECTOR,
WITH HIS NOURA MOROCCAN HIGH-
PILE WOOL RUG COLLECTION

THERE ARE PIECES THAT FURNISH A HOME.
AND THOSE THAT DEFINE IT.

EDITOR'S LETTER

Game of two halves

My first personal encounter with Italian architect and designer Fabio Novembre was rather unorthodox. Wallpaper* magazine had always admired his work and considered him a leading light in contemporary design, but when, in 2008, he produced a pair of 'reinventions' of Verner Panton's 'S' chair that resembled male and female backsides, we couldn't resist the opportunity to give them a critical, ahem, slap. In fact, Wallpaper* bestowed on them the honour of being 'worst design of the year' in our annual Design Awards issue (W*119).

Over the years, I have learned to expect grumpy correspondence, sometimes physical threats, from designers who've found themselves in that feature, but Fabio took it exceptionally well and got in touch with me to say how delighted he was to be recognised in such a way. In a remarkable gesture of joie de vivre, he even did us the honour of highlighting this accolade in an ad for his solo show at the Milan Triennale.

Fabio and I have stayed friends ever since, so I was excited to hear, a little over a year ago, that he had received an extraordinary commission from legendary football club AC Milan. Barbara Berlusconi had recently arrived at the helm of the *rossoneri* and wanted Fabio to refashion a Gino Valle-designed building in the Portello district into its new headquarters. The world of football is not renowned for its appetite for progressive design, so I knew this was a fascinating story to follow.

For months Fabio teased me with messages and sketches of his project, so it was a thrill finally to get a private view just before I flew back to London from Salone del Mobile last April. It had been a gruelling five days in Milan and I was a little the worse for wear, but to be shown around the not-quite-finished headquarters by Fabio, Barbara and long-time club chief Adriano Galliani (pictured in discussion with Fabio, above) left me in high spirits. See Pierpaolo Ferrari's stunning photographs and read JJ Martin's profile on page 054.

Hats off to Fabio for giving a bold and fresh face to such a classic global brand, and to Barbara for her big and brave vote of confidence in design. This project is testament to the power and ever-growing reach of contemporary design, and a fitting opener to our annual Design Directory issue. Enjoy the magazine.
Tony Chambers, Editor-in-Chief

Grand Suite. The true luxury of living. This sofa makes a statement about what is particularly private. Large, soft cushions and details in best saddle leather, masterly crafted. Pure elegance for what really is precious – your private life. Design: EOOS.

Walter Knoll AG & Co. KG
www.walterknoll.de
info@walterknoll.de
T +49(0)70 32/208-0

こんにちは

SU by NENDO
Su is a Japanese word meaning simple or unadorned. Made in
America from repurposed, reclaimed and upcycled waste.

New addition

A formulaic chair has the bow-wow factor

Design a piece of furniture inspired by a mathematical formula: this is the challenge that Italian furniture manufacturer Gufram posed to theoretical physicist Tullio Regge back in 1967. The mathematician-turned-designer delivered the 'Detecma' chair, the first piece of furniture ever designed on a computer; its hybrid form and avant-garde concept made it a design gem, which until now has been quietly hidden away in museum archives. But later this year, Gufram is relaunching 'Detecma' with a few unmathematical tweaks. The shape remains identical to Regge's original, but this modern-day rendition comes in six gradated colour versions that between them cover pretty much the entire spectrum. *www.gufram.it*

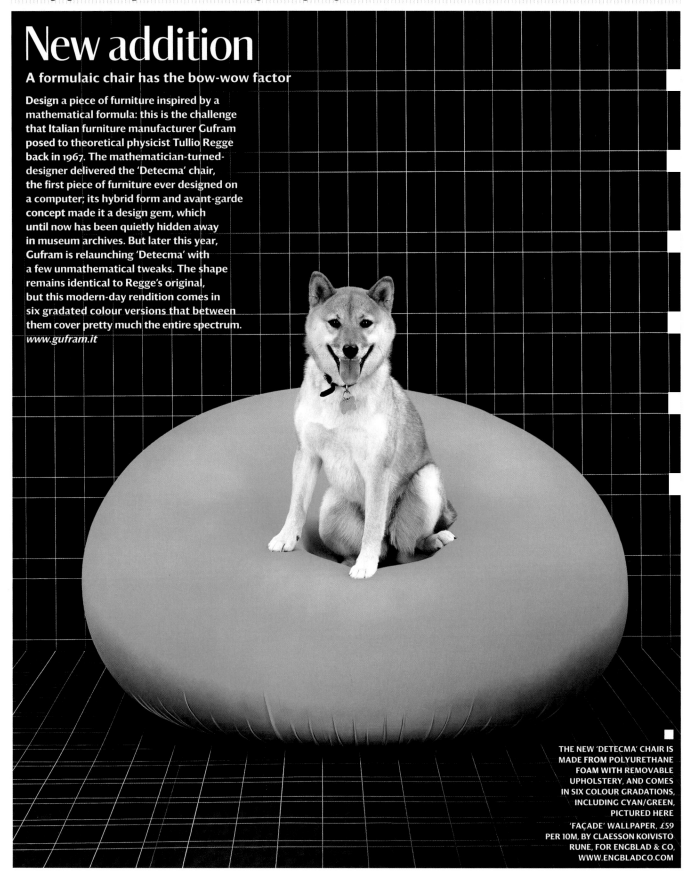

THE NEW 'DETECMA' CHAIR IS MADE FROM POLYURETHANE FOAM WITH REMOVABLE UPHOLSTERY, AND COMES IN SIX COLOUR GRADATIONS, INCLUDING CYAN/GREEN, PICTURED HERE

'FAÇADE' WALLPAPER, £59 PER 10M, BY CLAESSON KOIVISTO RUNE, FOR ENGBLAD & CO, WWW.ENGBLADCO.COM

Model: Kenny

PHOTOGRAPHY: LUKE & NIK WRITER: ROSA BERTOLI

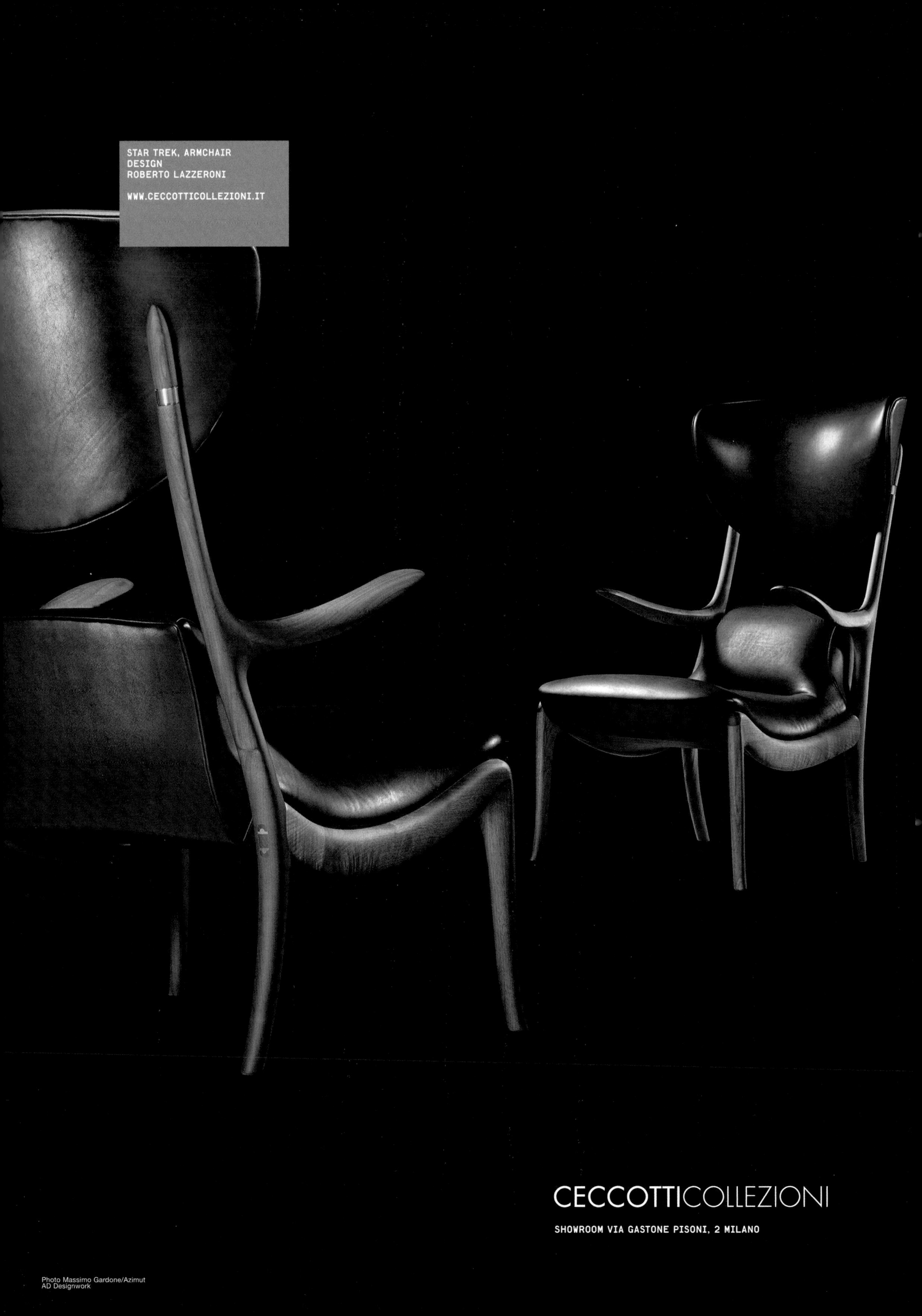
STAR TREK, ARMCHAIR
DESIGN
ROBERTO LAZZERONI
WWW.CECCOTTICOLLEZIONI.IT
CECCOTTICOLLEZIONI
SHOWROOM VIA GASTONE PISONI, 2 MILANO
Photo Massimo Gardone/Azimut
AD Designwork

Clay time

Once the domain of rustic Mediterranean villa floors, terracotta has a crafty new role as the main material in a series of strikingly modern designs

01 'Tierras' tiles, from €10 each, by Patricia Urquiola, for Mutina, from Domus

02 'Torei' table, from £650, by Luca Nichetto, for Cassina

03 Lens box, £32, by Thomas Jenkins, for Wrong for Hay

04 'W103' table lamp, €567, by Inga Sempé, for Wästberg

05 'Geo' box, price on request, by Hay

06 'Terracotta' pendant light, €200, by Tomas Kral, for PCM

07 'Pourer' pot, DKK400 (€53), by Benjamin Hubert, for Menu

08 Terracotta pitcher, bowl and platter, from £56, by Reiko Kaneko, for SCP

09 Flower pot, €100, by Atelier Polyhedre

10 Caddy in clay, DKK250 (€33), by Afteroom, for Menu

11 'Stomach' flower pot, €300, by Atelier Polyhedre

For stockists, see page 224

■ TEA AND SYMMETRY

Tucked away in the forests of one of the Sacred Mountains of China, the Tianzhoushan Tea House, in Anhui province, was built as an homage to Chinese painting. Designed by Sino-Swiss practice Archiplein, which featured in our 2013 Architects Directory, this concrete visitor centre was designed to work in harmony with the site's dramatic surroundings. 'Here, building and nature are not seen as two separate systems,' says Francis Jacquier of Archiplein. 'They are approached as an integrated whole where the architecture is by no means the main focus point of the composition.' The structure spans 1,000 sq m, following the landscape's contours down to the shores of a manmade mountain lake, and features large, irregular openings. Located a walk away from the nearest village, it includes a restaurant overlooking the lake, and makes the perfect pit stop for summer hikers.
www.archiplein.com

PHOTOGRAPHY: ANDREA GARUTI, FRÉDÉRIC HENRIQUES INTERIORS: EMMA MOORE WRITER: ELLIE STATHAKI

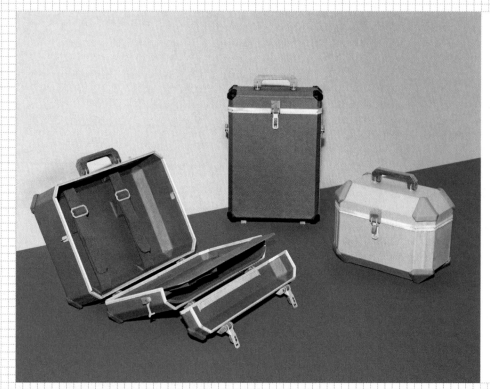

■ GOING DUTCH

Johan Bouman and Pieter Franssens, the Dutch owners of Château de la Resle in Montigny, near Auxerre, recently launched a range of hotel merchandise to beat all hotel merchandise. Having first recruited a collective of Dutch design talent, the pair presented the range at Salone del Mobile. On show were tablecloths by Carolina Wilcke and Reinier Bosch, and glassware by Daphna Laurens, as well as egg cups, butter dishes and chopping boards, versions of which are all on active duty at the château. We took a particular shine to Jeroen Wand's luggage collection (pictured), made in laminated paper and wood, but suitably robust and waterproof. Available at the château or online. *Limited-edition suitcase, €1,595; briefcase, €1,395; beauty case, €1,395, all by Jeroen Wand, for Château de la Resle, www.chateaudelaresle.com*

CASE STUDIES

The design aficionado's guide to getting away from it all

■ PACKING A PUNCH

In an old garage by the Meguro river, the Best Packing Store has Tokyo's top selection of everything you need for your next weekend out of town. Takayuki Minami, of creative agency Alpha, has applied his trademark minimal design approach, making good use of exposed plywood, chalkboard-painted pegboards, ropes and the like for an almost DIY-feel interior. This is nicely offset with the good-quality travel merchandise that includes stainless steel cups and canisters from Klean Kanteen, nose-hair clippers from Zwilling and original Lorinza bags. *www.bestpackingstore.com*

01 **02** **03**

TRAVELLING COMPANIONS

The standout packing simplifier at travel store Flight001 is the Spacepak range (1), a selection of bags designed to compartmentalise and compress clothes, toiletries and shoes, meaning over-packers can now load up to their heart's content. Tangled electrical cords, meanwhile, are the traveller's nemesis. No matter how tightly you wind them up, they tend to unravel and knot. With chargers, adaptors and headphones all proving vital travel gear, LA design collective This is Ground has devised a leather cord holder, the Cordito (2), which apparently takes its design cues from the humble burrito. Finally, Piquadro's essential weekend bag (3) features three compartments and six pockets, as well as an inner-garment bag that unzips from the outer case, making suits and formal shirts painlessly portable.
F1 Spacepak, from $28, by Flight001, www.flight001.com; Cordito, $40, by This is Ground, thisisground.com; weekend bag, £275, by Piquadro, www.piquadro.com

PHOTOGRAPHY: LUKE & NIK WRITERS: NICK COMPTON, JENS H JENSEN, ELIZABETH HUTTON

Fragrant offerings

ECAL's design students get a nose for perfume

What happens when students on one of design's most prestigious master's courses are introduced to one of the world's most admired perfumers? Francis Kurkdjian, head of the eponymous fragrance house, was invited to brief ECAL's Master of Advanced Studies in Design for Luxury and Craftsmanship with a history of his brand and an olfactory overview at his Paris store. ECAL then enlisted Jaime Hayon to guide the students' scent-inspired design ideas. The successful projects range from the practical, such as a fan by Luc Beaussart (top left) and scent strips by Hongchao Wang (top right), to the poetic and playful, such as a drop-shaped diffuser from Rachel Suming (bottom right) and Anouk Meyer's nature-inspired diffuser (bottom left). They will be shown during Paris Design Week and considered for inclusion in the Maison Francis Kurkdjian range. *Grand Palais, Paris, 6-13 September, www.franciskurkdjian.com, www.ecal.ch*

INCOMING | JOHN WEICH

SOUND WAVES

Research has proved that gadget noises can't be too inhuman because a lack of familiarity tunes us out. This is why, despite access to gazillions of sound bites, our microwaves still tend to go ping and our phones mostly ring. Sound engineers like to soothe us into new technologies with noises we know (the smartphone tap, the digital camera shutter), but for the next wave of gadgetry, you'd think they'd be eagerly plotting a revolution of avant-garde noises. Nothing could be further from the truth. From blenders and washing machines to portable fans, appliances are being programmed not with music or sound effects but with the most soothing sound of all: silence. Turns out the best way to make us feel at home with new technology is to 'de-beep' it altogether.

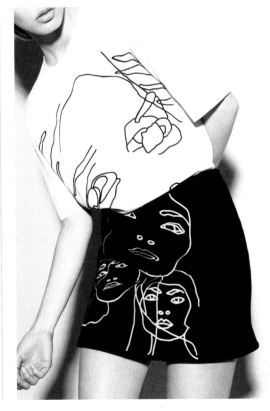

■ QUITE A DRAW

While many designers sharpened their edge by emblazoning slogans on their separates this season, Stella McCartney turned to the doodles of British artist Gary Hume. It's not the first time McCartney has sought out the pared-back figurative art of her friend Hume - in fact, the very drawings that featured on this spring's runway were conceived for her first solo show back in 2002. Reworked into this season's heavily textured collection, represented in optic white threadwork embroidery on black wool coats, in jacquard tops and oversized intarsia knits, the second life feels as fresh and relevant as the first. *Top, £645; skirt, £725, both by Stella McCartney, www.stellamccartney.com*

Model: Marloes at Elite London.
Hair: Ranelle Chapman using Bumble and bumble.
Make-up: Nobuko Maekawa using YSL Beauté.
Set design: Jude Singleton for Settrade.co.uk

SHADES OF GREY

Monochromatic magnificence reigns over the pre-fall menswear collections

↖

JACKET, £1,860; TROUSERS, £575, BOTH BY LOUIS VUITTON. PIN, £120, BY LANVIN, FROM MR PORTER. RING, MODEL'S OWN

↑

COAT, £1,310; SUIT, £1,310, BOTH BY GUCCI. SHOES, £370, BY EMPORIO ARMANI. PIN, £115, BY LANVIN, FROM MR PORTER. BROOCH, £40, BY CARVEN, FROM OKI-NI

→

JUMPER, £425, BY CALVIN KLEIN COLLECTION

←

JUMPER, £610; SHIRT, £350; TROUSERS, £450, ALL BY DIOR HOMME

FOR STOCKISTS, SEE PAGE 224

Model: Emmanuel O'Brien at Models 1. Hair: Yoshitaka Miyazaki at Untitled Artists using L'Oréal Professionnel Paris

PHOTOGRAPHY: LENA C EMERY FASHION: MATHEW STEVENSON-WRIGHT

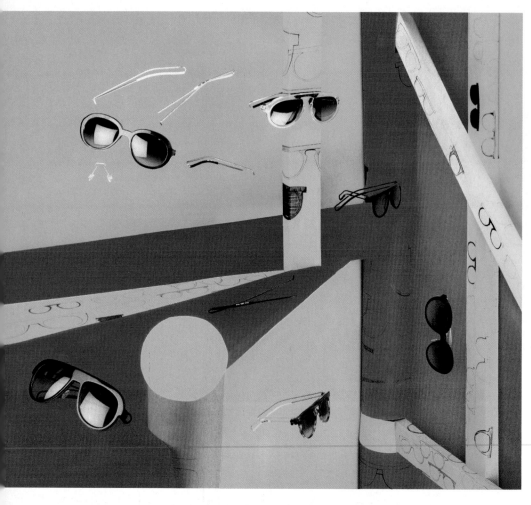

Bright eyes

Eyewear goes modular for infinitely more specs appeal

Modularity is the design buzzword du jour. And eyewear is at the forefront of the trend. Nendo has just launched a collection of Magne-hinge glasses which, as the name suggests, replaces the screw in the hinge with a magnet, allowing glasses to be easily customised with differently coloured temples. A new range of sunglasses by Swiss firm Sol Sol Ito (pictured) offers even more modular behaviour, with easily interchangeable temples and nose pieces, allowing for restyling and a perfect fit. The range is the work of Monica Fink, a design engineer-turned-sculptor, and Sandra Kaufmann, co-head of advanced industrial design at Zurich University. The frames, which click together, come in five designs and three colours, with hand-polished acetate fronts and steel temples. *From €340, www.solsolito.com*

■ COSMETIC TREATMENT

Italian beauty brand Madina got more than it bargained for after appointing UK design firm Doshi Levien to create a new interior for its shops. 'When it comes to make-up stores, the product is the interior,' says the firm's Nipa Doshi. 'So it made sense to address the packaging and logo to give a consistent identity.' Madina, formerly the Milanese retail arm of make-up manufacturer Intercos, was bought by the Percassi group, owner of the Kiko make-up brand, in 2012. Now it plans to open up to 70 new stores in Italy and as many in France. To facilitate the roll-out, Doshi Levien designed the canvas of the store, then freestanding furniture - even shelves and mirrors are clip on rather than built in. The flagship opens on Milan's via Dante in July. *www.doshilevien.com, www.madina.it*

■ BURIED TREASURE

Milanese jeweller Lia Di Gregorio loves pearls, but often keeps them concealed. 'By inverting the position of what has always been considered the most precious element in a classical jewel, it becomes intriguing,' she says. Her pieces are also lovely to wear: the secret pearls roll smoothly against the skin. *Ring, €2,500, by Lia Di Gregorio, from Dover Street Market, shop.doverstreetmarket.com*

PHOTOGRAPHY: EMILE BARRET, DANIELE DE CAROLIS, LUKE & NIK WRITERS: NICK COMPTON, EMMA MOORE, CARAGH MCKAY

THE HQ OF NIASCA PORTOFINO,
RENOVATED BY ARCHITECT
LUCA CIPELLETTI, BELOW,
WITH ARTIST DAVID TREMLETT

Collective growth

An ingenious co-op is selling foodstuffs to fund the revival of Portofino's hillsides and its own HQ

The small Ligurian town of Portofino may be best known for its port crammed with yachts the size of city blocks and glittering shops selling €2,000 handbags, but its real beauty lies on the people-free hills above the commercial frenzy. Known to the locals as Il Monte, the slope is a patchwork of wild foliage and agricultural plots, some of which have fallen into disrepair. Two years ago, a group of residents formed a collective called Niasca Portofino, which began to rent pieces of abandoned land and revive them. Since its inception, Niasca has saved or replanted hundreds of olive trees, lemon trees and grape vines, and has planted out countless herbs and spices that flourish in the local climate.

'There are enough stores, restaurants and boats in Portofino,' says Simona Mussini, owner of the port's Ö Magazin restaurant and one of the partners in Niasca. 'We wanted to do something different.' Working with her sister Emilia, who co-owns the restaurant, and other partners – local builder Mino

Viacava and entrepreneurs Luca Baffigo and Alberto Grunstein – Mussini and Niasca have transformed the local agricultural output into olive oil, wine, lemonade, jam, pesto and tomato sauce. And the proceeds from the sales fund the land's regeneration. Now their environmental-social mission has expanded to the restoration of an abandoned building in Portofino, where the co-op's newest activities, including cooking classes, wine tastings and private dinners, will take place.

Located at the very top of the port, across from the insider's favourite, the Trattoria Concordia restaurant, the new HQ was once the most run-down edifice in town. 'It was just a pile of rubble, really,' says Luca Cipelletti, the Milan-based architect behind the renovation. 'No one wanted to come up to this part of the town.'

The region's stiff architectural stipulations meant that Cipelletti could only faithfully restore what was once there. But he brought on board English artist David Tremlett, »

PHOTOGRAPHY: DANILO SCARPATI WRITER: JJ MARTIN

LEFT, INTERIORS PAINTED
BY TREMLETT, WITH OLIVE-WOOD
FURNISHINGS, AND TRAPEZIUM
LIGHTS BY CIPELLETTI AND LIGHTING
DESIGNER ALBERTO PASETTI

BELOW, PORTOFINO, AT THE
FOOT OF ONE OF THE HILLSIDES
REGENERATED BY NIASCA

Cipelletti. 'But that tradition was lost in the 20th century. The idea was to bring art back to the façades but in a modern way.'

While the exterior was painted by Tremlett's trusted handyman, the interior features raw-powder-pigment artworks that Tremlett rubbed into the walls himself. The wall art is complemented by Cipelletti's interiors, which make use of local materials, with Bedonia stone floors and veiny olive-wood tables and cabinets. The trapezium graphic has been incorporated into steel door knobs, light sconces and chandeliers.

The new HQ not only introduces the public to Niasca's activities, but serves as a gateway to Il Monte, with tours led along the pathways directly behind the building. Inside, the ground floor features a *frantoio*, where olives are crushed to make oil, as well as 19th-century farm tools, all of which come from the hillside 100m away. Upstairs, two bedrooms and a bath provide temporary lodging for Niasca friends and supporters.

'All of this has been put together for the love of the land,' says Cipelletti, who has been coming to Portofino since he was a small boy.

'At the beginning, all the locals just stared at us,' says Mussini of Niasca's initiatives. But eventually they coaxed residents into participating with plot sharing. 'Now they get it and want to be a part of it.' ✳
www.niascaportofino.it

best known for temporal works he draws on the walls of museums, galleries and ruins; he has embellished Tate Britain's staircase and, with artist Sol LeWitt, a chapel in Barolo.

Using an abstracted trapezium graphic, Tremlett added a new geometry to the surface of the building's exterior with a Portofino-friendly palette of earthy reds, ochres and greens. 'You've got this building going up the hill, so there was already this stepping concept,' the artist says. 'The lines were a way of terracing the building and unifying its three structures.'

Though the architectural lines of the building remain traditional, this is the first time in a hundred years that anyone has brought change to the codified structures of Portofino. As a consequence, the building looks unlike anything else in town.

'From the 17th century, there was always something artistic in the façades of traditional Ligurian architecture,' says

BOCCI 28

THE VINSON VIEW

Quality maniac and master shopper Nick Vinson on the who, what, when, where and why

WELCOME MR. VINSON

Now that's good service

How to ensure you never need to complain again

Arriving at the fairground for this year's Salone del Mobile, armed with my brand new Red Card – giving fast-track access for VIPs and selected press – I was thrilled to find dedicated turnstiles and check-in desks. Flying through the entry process gave me more time with the exhibitors. While I can't take total credit for this improvement, my dinner date some six months earlier was Claudio Luti, president of Cosmit, who runs the fair. I told him how painful it had been to get into the fair in 2013, when I arrived at the east door, with no press desk in sight and around one kilometre to walk to the south door to get help.

Of course, you won't always have the ear of the boss, but there's a fine art to complaining. It's essential to think about why you are doing it. Do you really care or are you just pissed off? It's so much easier just to walk away, save your breath and take your business elsewhere. Complaining well is time consuming and almost like giving out free advice. I won't bother unless the business in question is one that I want to (or must) return to. I've had issues at Chateau Marmont in LA, the Park Hyatt in Milan and the Standard in New York, yet they listen and learn, so I go back and we all win.

Twitter is a new tool for some pretty swift action. Brands like to protect their reputation, and a complaint tweeted is a complaint dealt with. I learnt this having suffered tedious and tacky piano playing spoiling an otherwise perfect evening in the garden at the Four Seasons in Florence. My tweet was replied to within minutes and the hotel was soon in touch. The same happened with Singapore Airlines. When I boarded one of their 'vintage' jets in Auckland there wasn't a single flat bed in sight. But they were falling over themselves for the rest of the journey to make up for letting their reputation down.

Constructive criticism gets you much more than angry ranting, and it's so satisfying when things improve. When I returned to London from Milan recently, my luggage failed to arrive. Before I even left the airport, British Airways' help-desk messages started to ping on my mobile with the first of many updates – arriving all day – until I had a call from a driver who was happy to be diverted to a local restaurant that same night, and deliver me my bags, all without my making a single phone call or being put on hold even once. On another occasion, I arrived without bags in a Beijing hotel for a long weekend. There I was contacted by a woman who introduced herself and said: 'My job today is to make sure you fly with British Airways again.' Needless to say, she did and I do. ✱

 Home comforts

A year after being rescued by Gucci, Richard Ginori, the Florentine porcelain manufacturer established in 1735, reopens the doors of its flagship store in Florence's via Rondinelli 17r. If all goes to plan we could see some Gucci tableware in 2015.

Top flock

The crowd pleaser at Milan's Salone was Marni's Animal House, a mix of collectable Colombian-made donkeys, giraffes, ostriches, rabbits, ducks and flamingoes.

ILLUSTRATOR: DANAE DIAZ

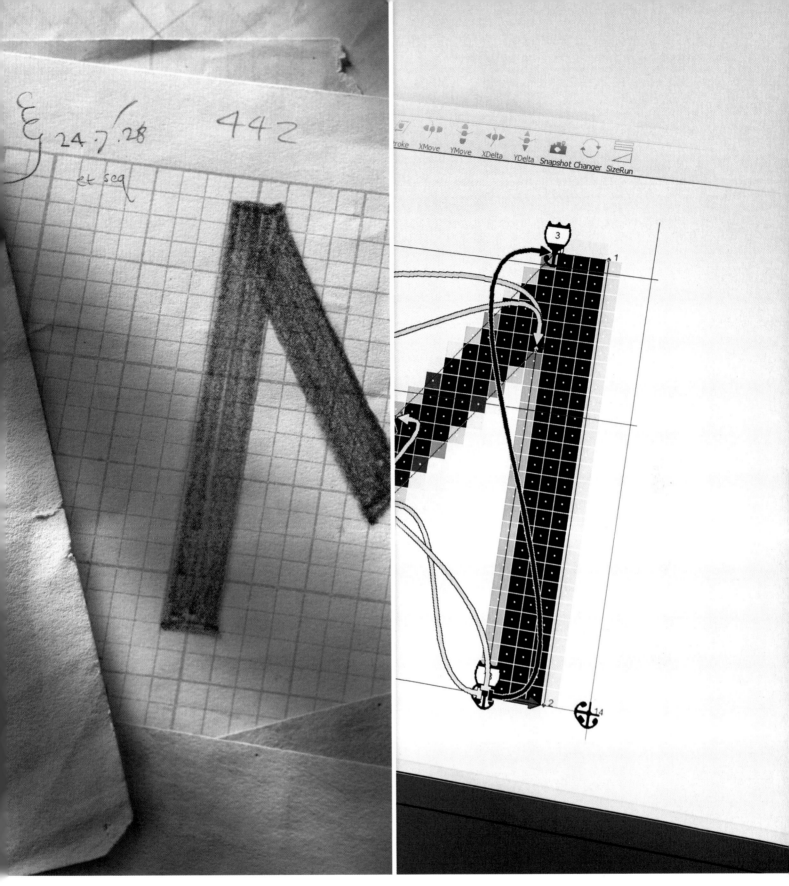

Legendary type design before digital.
And after.

Bringing Eric Gill's hand-sketched drawings to life online required an equally meticulous obsession with detail, and Monotype's Edge™ tuning technology. How will you build your next masterpiece as tools move from pencil to pixel?

Monotype

Dream team

An irresistible hybrid of haute-heiress and Milanese marketing savant, Barbara Berlusconi - just 29 years old and the lone female boss in Italian football - has commissioned architect Fabio Novembre to design a radical new HQ for her AC Milan club: a palace of pilgrimage for fans of the *rossoneri*, and a sporting vernacular all her own

PHOTOGRAPHY: PIERPAOLO FERRARI WRITER: JJ MARTIN

ARCHITECT AND DESIGNER
FABIO NOVEMBRE AND
VICE-PRESIDENT AND CEO
OF AC MILAN BARBARA
BERLUSCONI IN THE EXECUTIVE
BOARDROOM OF CASA MILAN,
THE FOOTBALL CLUB'S NEW
HEADQUARTERS IN PORTELLO

T hough they may have fallen to Atlético Madrid in the European Champions League quarter finals, and Juventus are dominant on the domestic front, AC Milan will record one very significant home win this year: the inauguration of Casa Milan, the football club's new home-town headquarters. Located in Portello, a redevelopment hot spot around the former Fiera Milano trade-fair space, the HQ is set in a gleaming red and black building with 9,000 sq m of hi-tech space designed by architect Fabio Novembre.

After half a century of being crammed into a disjointed building in via Turati, where various floors and offices were acquired over the years, Casa Milan is the first space fully dedicated to the football club's management, employees and operations. And, uniquely, it also caters to the die-hard Milan fans, local and international, who are welcomed into the six-storey building's new store, restaurant and museum.

'No other football club in the world has a brand hub like this,' says Barbara Berlusconi, who shares the title of vice president and CEO of AC Milan with long-time club chief Adriano Galliani. 'We call this Casa Milan because the concept is about our home. We aren't just a

THIS PAGE, EACH SLICE OF THE CORRIDOR FROM THE CAR PARK TO THE RECEPTION GRADATES FROM DARK GREY TO WHITE, AND IS LIT BY A SERIES OF LED LIGHTS

MODEL, THROUGHOUT, WEARS T-SHIRT, £1,775; SKIRT, £1,125; SHOES, £485, ALL BY TOD'S, WWW.TODS.COM

OPPOSITE, NOVEMBRE AT CASA MILAN'S SECURITY BOOTH. THE FIST SCULPTURE IS A PROTOTYPE BY THE ARCHITECT FOR THE FIVE GIANT FOOTBALLING FIGURES THAT ADORN THE BUILDING'S ROOF

Fashion: Francesca Cefis

Model: Ria Serebriakova at Why Not Model Management

Hair & make-up: Lorenzo Zavatta

Producer: Federico Delle Piane

club, but a family. We want to entertain, give a service to clients, and make them feel part of the club.'

Casa Milan is the brainchild of Berlusconi, who now leads the club's commercial arm, while Galliani maintains power over the players on the pitch. With a controversial, carefully dissected start to her career at the club (she is, after all, owner Silvio Berlusconi's daughter), Berlusconi is waging two uphill battles in Italy. Aged 29, not only is she an exceptionally young voice within Italy's power circles, but in a sport dominated by macho males, she's a lone female boss. 'My father owns the club – that helps,' she's quick to point out about her rise to the top. 'And it's not that impressive. I started everything young.' Still, not every heiress is so keen and quick to take advantage of their

inherited opportunities. After studying philosophy at the University of Vita-Salute San Raffaele in Milan and graduating with top honours, Berlusconi beefed up her business credentials with courses at Bocconi University. She joined the board of directors of her father's media holding company Fininvest in 2003 and made her first individual business investment in the Milanese art gallery, Cardi Black Box, in 2009. In 2011 she joined the board of directors of AC Milan, and began to handle business development for the club.

When she was anointed co-CEO of the club, Berlusconi ignored the tabloid brouhaha and kept her head focused on business. She's now cut the ribbon on Casa Milan, the first concrete evidence of her commercial ambitions for the club. 'We didn't want to do brand-slapping,' says Berlusconi in no-nonsense, beautifully clipped English. 'Many teams just focus on their retail departments. We wanted something that really had the Milan culture in it.'

To harness the city's ties to fashion, food and design, Berlusconi enlisted Novembre for the headquarters' design and concept development. 'He's one of the designers that best represents Italy and the taste of »

'My father owns the club – that helps,' she's quick to point out about her rise to the top

'In a way, it's like a cathedral. People want to come and see and say, "That's my team." The piazza is a place for celebration'

Milan,' she explains. 'Plus the passion that he has for football made him able to grasp our ideas and values and to help us explode them.'

The Lecce-born, Milan-based architect and designer, who has 'been playing soccer since birth', jumped on the project with all the enthusiasm of a card-carrying AC Milan fan. 'There's so much potential for AC Milan as a brand,' says Novembre. 'The name is a very powerful tool that can be used to great effect.'

AC Milan's home was not a simple project. The building itself, shaped like a 3D polygon with a diagonally slanted roof, was designed nearly 15 years ago by Italian architect Gino Valle as one of three buildings off via Aldo Rossi. Valle passed away in 2003 before seeing his buildings completed, and before knowing one of Europe's great football teams would call one of them home.

'In terms of urban development, this is a very interesting area, but everything in Italy is so fucking slow,' says Novembre with his trademark frankness. 'It's a miracle we got this done in one year.'

Unable to change the building's preexisting lines, Novembre 'tried to make the façade come alive'. He wrapped the exterior with red and black waves using 3M Scotchcal film, and placed five giant-scale human sculptures along the roof perimeter. Cut from flat aluminium, the figures appear to sprint up the incline, the last one triumphantly kicking a ball off the edge.

Though now out of Milan's city centre, the football club is significantly closer to the heartbeat of San Siro, the stadium it shares with rival local team Inter Milan (and which Berlusconi also has plans to completely redesign before 2018). One side of the new building features a four-storey video screen that will broadcast FIFA World Cup Brazil matches this summer, and future Milan games for the mob of fans who can fit into the massive 25,000 sq m piazza below.

On the ground floor, a 450 sq m restaurant called Cucina Milanello has been modelled after AC Milan's famous sports centre, where the team's athletes eat traditional but healthy food. In addition, the restaurant features Kvadrat stools, 'Cyborg' chairs by Magis, Flos lighting, and TV screens for non-stop football.

Inside the HQ, Novembre covered the walls with images from AC Milan's history, but stretched them in Photoshop to give the illusion of abstracted speed. The ground floor also has a new club store. The second floor houses Milan Lab, where team players receive medical exams, while the third floor has an employee-only bar. Chairs designed by Ron Arad and Philippe Starck populate the bar, while Magis chairs and Kartell tables fill the conference rooms.

Below the building is a new interactive museum built to celebrate the club's 115-year history as seven-time winners of the European Cup/Champions League, with trophies, memorabilia and a hall of fame.

'In a way, it's like a cathedral,' says Novembre of Casa Milan. 'People want to come and see and say: "That's my team." The piazza is a place for celebration and winning. This is for the future of the team.' ✱

THIS PAGE, NOVEMBRE AND
BERLUSCONI BESIDE SOME OF THE
AC MILAN ARCHIVE IMAGERY
THAT NOVEMBRE STRETCHED IN
PHOTOSHOP TO FEATURE ON
THE INTERIOR WALLS

OPPOSITE, NOVEMBRE ON ONE OF
HIS DESIGNS IN A BREAK-OUT SPACE,
WITH FABRIC-COVERED COLUMNS
AND FLOOR TILES BY LEA CERAMICHE

London has seen the opening of a slew of interesting hotels recently, from the Rosewood on High Holborn in Frieze week last year to the high-flying Shangri-La at the Shard (see W*183). The latest jewel in the city's crown is from Morgans Hotel Group, which is launching its first Mondrian hotel outside the US. The hotel is located on South Bank in Warren Platner's iconic 1978 Sea Containers House (see W*44). Its presence on the Thames Path links it to riverside spaces such as the Royal Festival Hall, the National Theatre, Tate Modern and culinary destination Borough Market. It's a sought-after location, and Morgans knew just what to do with it. The interiors are by Design Research Studio, the firm under the creative direction of designer Tom Dixon, who, for his first hotel, took cues from the building's architect – known for everything from the Window on the World restaurant in New York's World Trade Center to a celebrated collection of furniture for Knoll – while also paying tribute to its sea-faring heritage by preserving original details such as Sea Containers' reception desk in the hotel's spa. The dramatic entrance is flanked by a 68m copper hull, which extends into the lobby, before tapering off into the riverside restaurant. Also on the ground floor, the Dandelyan cocktail bar, overseen by barman Ryan Chetiyawardana (W*178), is characterised by the use of bold green, accented with a marble bar, brass detailing and parquet flooring. The 359 guest rooms feature a palette of subtle greys and whites, with bespoke furniture by Dixon complementing the designer's signature wingback chair. Thirty of the 43 suites have river views, but the panoramic vistas from the rooftop bar are set to be the biggest attraction.

20 Upper Ground, SE1, tel: 44.20 3747 1000, www.morganshotelgroup.com. Rates: from £195

Shore leave

In a former shipping HQ, London's Mondrian makes a tempting berth

PHOTOGRAPHY: CATHERINE HYLAND WRITER: LAUREN HO

THIS PAGE, THE INTERIORS
BY TOM DIXON'S DESIGN
RESEARCH STUDIO REFERENCE
THE BUILDING'S NAUTICAL
HERITAGE. A COPPER-CLAD HULL
– ITS SHINGLES HAND-ROLLED
AND HELD TOGETHER BY MORE
THAN 160,000 NAILS – SWEEPS
THROUGH THE ENTRANCE

OPPOSITE, THE GREEN-HUED
DANDELYAN COCKTAIL BAR

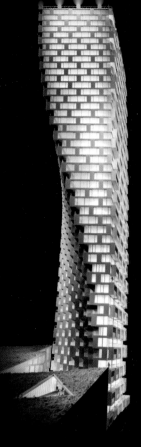

DEPARTURE INFO

Zhengzhou shapes up, where to be the centre of attention in Beirut, plus this month's best new urban hotels

High flyer

LE MÉRIDIEN, ZHENGZHOU, CHINA →

Rising elegantly above the urban chaos of Zhengzhou, in China's Henan province, is this 25-storey steel and glass structure, home to the new Le Méridien hotel. Shanghai-based architecture and design firm Neri & Hu has transformed a concrete shell into an angular tower of irregular, stacked boxes that cantilever, seemingly haphazardly. Inside, the design makes for soaring heights and open views. The 350-room hotel is built around a central, four-storey atrium, which, inspired by the nearby Longmen Caves (where Buddhist art is carved into limestone), combines sandstone and walnut with recessed, green-tinted windows that link to other public spaces. Elsewhere, mirror-ceilinged corridors and bespoke chandeliers add to the visual stimulation. **Lauren Ho**
No 1188 Zhongzhou Avenue, Jinshui District, tel: 86.371 5599 8888, starwoodhotels.com. Rates: from RMB1,251 ($200)

Enter the arena

STEREO KITCHEN, BEIRUT, LEBANON ←

Beirut-based architect Paul Kaloustian's latest project, a dramatic rooftop bar and restaurant overlooking central Beirut, the port and beyond, is a place to see and be seen. Stereo Kitchen is divided into two areas: an indoor space ringed by gently tiered concrete seats or dividers, and an outdoor wrap-around terrace. Inside is loud and energetic, while outside is quiet and contemplative. Chef Fouad Kassab's mezze-style menu offers international trends, from mini-burgers with caramelised foie gras to white-fish ceviche. The restaurant caters to voyeurs and wallflowers alike; the deliberately tight tiers make interaction imperative, while the panoramic views of the Eastern Mediterranean will compel even the modest to feel a little like a god.
Warren Singh-Bartlett
Rooftop, Modern Building, rue Pasteur, Gemmayze, tel: 96.1 71 366377

ARTFUL LODGER

Enjoy luxury at the touch of a button in Paris or swim to an underwater soundtrack in New York: this month's best new urban hotels

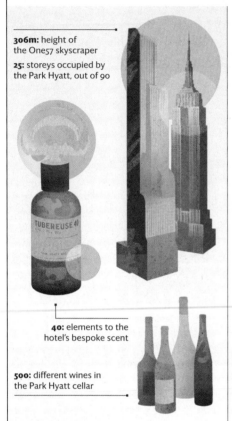

306m: height of the One57 skyscraper

25: storeys occupied by the Park Hyatt, out of 90

40: elements to the hotel's bespoke scent

500: different wines in the Park Hyatt cellar

Tokyo infusion

ANDAZ TOKYO, JAPAN

The upcoming 2020 Olympic Games in Tokyo has resulted in a surge of new hotel plans and openings. Hyatt is betting on the offbeat Toranomon business area – currently undergoing tremendous redevelopment – where it will launch Japan's first Andaz hotel. The boutique offering occupies the top six floors of the 247m-high Toranomon Hills skyscraper complex. The interiors have been created by Hyatt regular Tony Chi and Tokyoite Shinichiro Ogata, who is known for his simple yet sophisticated design aesthetic. Comprising 164 rooms, each fitted with large round bathtubs, Hokkaido walnut finishes and providing panoramic city vistas, the hotel has easy access to neighbourhoods such as Ginza, Marunouchi and Roppongi. Striking artworks by local and international artists punctuate the public spaces, while the rooftop bar, inspired by Katsura Rikyū – the most beautiful of Japan's imperial villas – comes with classic touches such as a sunken *irori* hearth in which water is boiled in the way of traditional tea houses. **Jens H Jensen** *1-23-4 Toranomon, tel: 81.3 6830 1212, andaztokyo.com. Rates: from ¥48,000 ($7,696)*

20: stonemasons to restore the interiors

3: weeks to repair each flower cascade

800: hand-blown leaves for the lobby chandelier

1.7m: height of a Peninsula door lion

4.6 tonnes: weight of a signature statue

Sound space

PARK HYATT NEW YORK, US

The Park Hyatt group has pulled out all the stops to create an impressive setting for its first New York outpost and global flagship. Occupying the first 25 floors of the recently developed 90-storey One57 skyscraper (designed by Paris-based architect Christian de Portzamparc), the 210-room hotel is brimming with special touches, including 475 sq ft entry-level rooms, among the largest in the city, a wellness centre on the top floor, a collection of museum-quality artwork – by the likes of Rob Fischer, Ellsworth Kelly and Richard Serra – and an exclusive soundtrack for the pool, courtesy of the nearby Carnegie Hall, played through underwater speakers. The understated interiors are by go-to hospitality designers of the moment Yabu Pushelberg, while chef Sam Hazen, formerly of Veritas and Tao, is in charge of the restaurant. A final takeaway: the hotel provides New York brand Le Labo's Tubereuse 40-scented toiletries as a home town exclusive. **Pei-Ru Keh** *157 West 57th Street, tel: 1.646 774 1234, newyork.park.hyatt.com. Rates: from $915*

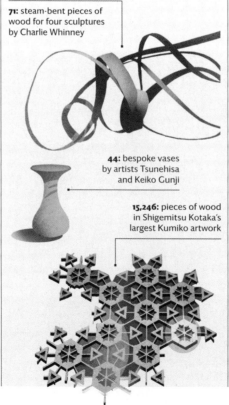

71: steam-bent pieces of wood for four sculptures by Charlie Whinney

44: bespoke vases by artists Tsunehisa and Keiko Gunji

15,246: pieces of wood in Shigemitsu Kotaka's largest Kumiko artwork

French leave

THE PENINSULA PARIS, FRANCE

We've been looking forward to the launch of The Peninsula Paris ever since the hotel group announced, six years ago, that it was going to make its European debut. Located a short walk away from the Arc de Triomphe, as well as historic monuments and key shopping districts, the 200-room property occupies a century-old building, which was previously the Hotel Majestic – one of the city's grandes dames. Both the façade and the interior have been meticulously restored by local craftsmen, and the hotel now comprises six dining areas, including a rooftop restaurant with views of the Eiffel Tower, a 22m indoor swimming pool and a lobby featuring a bespoke Lasvit chandelier made up of 800 individual hand-blown crystal leaves. With its own dedicated in-house technology team, The Peninsula Paris can safely say it has the world's most technologically customised rooms, where everything – from laundry collection to bathroom ambience – can be controlled at the touch of a button. **Lauren Ho** *19 Avenue Kléber, Paris, tel: 33.1 5812 2888, peninsula.com. Rates: from €695*

HOOP
adolini+simonini associati
2013

martinelliluce.com

THONET

New Showroom Amsterdam

www.thonet.de

DD 2014

Design Directory

The world's most inspiring
emerging architects, intriguing
new builds and innovative design,
plus a globetrotting round-up
of the finest new furniture
for every inch of your home

The W* House

Architecture

A NEW WINERY DESIGNED
BY SMILJAN RADIC FOR VIK
RETREATS IN MILLAHUE, CHILE.
THE RUNNING-WATER POOL
AT THE ENTRANCE, CREATED
WITH RADIC'S WIFE, SCULPTOR
MARCELA CORREA, HELPS
COOL THE WINERY'S
UNDERGROUND FACILITIES

SEE WALLPAPER.COM FOR
PHOTOGRAPHS OF RADIC'S
NEWLY COMPLETED SERPENTINE
PAVILION IN LONDON'S
KENSINGTON GARDENS

Rock solid

From this Chilean winery to London's new Serpentine Pavilion, architect Smiljan Radic is building a reputation with fabric roofs, fake ruins and a supporting cast of boulders

PHOTOGRAPHY: CRISTÓBAL PALMA WRITER: ELLIE STATHAKI

Iam not a creator of new shapes,' says Chilean architect Smiljan Radic, when asked about his design approach. It's true that, if anything, Radic's work, created using modern as well as natural and traditional materials and techniques, can feel at times strangely familiar. He works a lot with existing architectural and historical narratives and references, which he plays with and reappropriates. 'I always want to begin from a project that I thought about or saw before, or existing sketches, or architectural history.'

Radic's new design for the Serpentine Pavilion in London is nothing like the gallery's architecture programme has ever seen before. Featuring a translucent ring of glass-reinforced plastic, sitting on solid rocks, a reference to a modern-day Neolithic dolmen wouldn't feel amiss.

This is only the architect's second building outside his home country (Radic took part in the Austrian bus stops project featured in W*183). The Serpentine Pavilion is also one of Britain's most awaited summer commissions, assigned each year to an architect that hasn't built in the UK before.

It all started a few months ago, when Serpentine co-director Julia Peyton-Jones was travelling through South America for research. She met Radic in November 2013 and in early December the architect received a call announcing that he'd been selected for the commission. 'There's something of an architectural explosion happening in Chile right now, and Smiljan is one of the most interesting architects working there today,' says Peyton-Jones. 'Crucially, Smiljan brilliantly adapts his style and use of materials to every setting.'

For this project Radic decided to play with the idea of the folly, referencing Japanese temples and using large rocks as foundations. 'Follies have been used historically in gardens and parks to propose something extravagant,' he says. 'This is a fake ruin, but at the same time it proposes a continuity. Rocks are often used as decoration, but here they're the real foundation of the volume. You may initially think that this is part of the park, but it's really part of the building. It helps dissolve the limits between architecture and nature.'

The pavilion will act as a café, resting and meeting space, as well as a multi-use platform for events, although these functions were not the 'key' to the design solution, says Radic. 'In the end the commission is about creating a symbolic place,' he says. 'The design and the ambience around the site are more powerful than the function. It's about thinking about small-scale and global architecture, and opening up a discussion.'

One of the first projects that brought Radic to international attention was his Mestizo restaurant in Santiago, completed in 2007. It uses similar, large, solid rocks to support its roof. He's also completed several

PHOTOGRAPHY: LEON CHEW, HISAO SUZUKI

private houses (including his own in Santiago), which experiment with local construction techniques and different materials, from concrete and stone to fabric, earth and copper. A sculptural entry into the 2010 Venice Architecture Biennale, curated by Kazuyo Sejima, made of granite stone and perfumed cedar wood, and created with Radic's wife, artist Marcela Correa, drew further attention to the architect's unconventional work, which balances the minimal, the fantastical and the everyday.

His approach, he says, isn't about form. It's not even about materials, although he admits he likes playing with the ordinary and the ephemeral. The final shape of a structure comes second to the methods used in construction. He learned this working in Chile, where he feels the many opportunities for self-building allow scope for architects to do things differently.

This year is a key one for Radic. He's just won a competition to design a telecommunications tower in Chile and completed an extension for the Chilean Museum of Pre-Colombian Art in Santiago. He's also about to complete a winery project for Vik Retreats, some 200km south of Santiago, in Millahue. The commission went to Radic (as well as architect

RADIC (ABOVE) AND A RENDER OF HIS SERPENTINE PAVILION (LEFT). THE GLASS-REINFORCED PLASTIC SHELL WAS CAST AT THE NORTH YORKSHIRE WORKSHOP OF ENGINEERING FIRM STAGE ONE (ABOVE LEFT)

SERPENTINE PAVILIONS

Of the 15 pavilion commissions by the gallery since 2000, Radic is the second South American architect to be invited, after Oscar Niemeyer in 2003. The last five pavilions have been designed by:

SOU FUJIMOTO, 2013
....
HERZOG & DE MEURON AND AI WEIWEI, 2012
....
PETER ZUMTHOR, 2011
....
JEAN NOUVEL, 2010
....
KAZUYO SEJIMA AND RYUE NISHIZAWA, SANAA, 2009

Loreto Lyon) after a countrywide competition in 2007. Radic then spent a further three years refining the winning design.

The client wanted to work with a Chilean architect and Radic's solution spoke to their overall vision. 'It was important that the winery be integrated into the landscape, while also creating something that was pleasing, unique and innovative,' say Vik Retreats owners Alexander and Carrie Vik.

Set among rolling hills and sweeping valleys with the Andes in the distance, the winery stands out with a 130m x 40m fabric roof, which filters natural light into the building. The low structure makes use of a variety of surfaces and textures on ground level, while the main facilities are placed below ground, where the winery unfolds and the barrels are kept.

This is a design that aims to be sustainable and eco-friendly. The light entering through the fabric roof is enough for the interior to operate without artificial lighting, and a ground-level water feature is instrumental in the underground level's natural cooling. The approach is emblematic of Radic's design: smartly used, simple, everyday elements elevated to create sublime spaces. ★

Under Construction

A haven for the well-heeled pleasure seeker, the mountain town of Aspen is known for good skiing, even better après-ski, and the surrounding White River National Forest. Come August, it will add the polished programme of the Aspen Art Museum to its attractions, in a new 33,000 sq ft structure by 2014 Pritzker Architecture Prize winner Shigeru Ban.

Located in downtown Aspen, the building, a new home for the existing institution, founded in 1979, is Ban's first US museum. 'Right from the start of the selection process, Shigeru received the highest scores,' recalls Heidi Zuckerman Jacobson, the museum's CEO and director. 'He was up for several other museum projects at the time [2007], but as we were the first team to visit him in Tokyo and tour his projects, I think he was charmed by our commitment.'

The building's simple glass box structure exposes it to postcard-perfect surroundings on all fronts. Ban added another layer, literally, by draping a wooden screen over the glass façades. Reminiscent of his intricate paper and cardboard experimentations, the textured overlay is made from a durable, fire-resistant composite of wood and paper, reinforced with resin.

'Because the museum doesn't have collections, there are many different exhibitions – it's like a basket and you can put anything you like inside,' Ban explains. The building's public rooftop is accessible either via a glass lift or the three-level grand staircase, and showcases a sculpture garden set against unobstructed views of Ajax Mountain. 'Without going through the lobby, you can go up to the roof,' smiles Ban.

The new Aspen Art Museum will open with several heavy hitters – an unprecedented pairing of Yves Klein and David Hammons, and abstract painter Tomma Abts and Venice Biennale alumna Rosemarie Trockel. The unique rooftop exhibition space will feature a new project by Cai Guo-Qiang, while the first level will house the debut museum showing of Ban's humanitarian work, such as his Paper Partition System for the United Nations Commissioner for Refugees, created for victims of natural disasters in various versions from 2006 to 2011. It's a perfectly pitched opening for a perfectly placed museum. ✱
www.shigerubanarchitects.com. The museum opens on 9 August, tel: 1.970 925 8050, www.aspenartmuseum.org

SHIGERU BAN'S NEW
ART MUSEUM IN ASPEN,
COLORADO, IS SET AGAINST
THE SCENIC BACKDROP
OF AJAX MOUNTAIN.
THE ROOFTOP WILL HOST
A CAFÉ, SCREENING FACILITIES
AND A SCULPTURE GARDEN

ABOVE, THE LATTICED WOOD
SCREEN ON THE MUSEUM
WILL ALLOW GLIMPSES
OF THE SCENERY OUTSIDE

High culture

Aspen is the slightly off-piste location for a new art museum

PHOTOGRAPHY: LAURA WILSON WRITER: PEI-RU KEH

Design

ON DISPLAY IN HER LONDON
STUDIO ARE HUNDREDS OF
LUBNA CHOWDHARY'S BRIGHT
CERAMIC TILES, JUXTAPOSING
THOUSANDS OF COLOURS

OPPOSITE, CHOWDHARY
AT WORK IN HER STUDIO
DESIGNED BY DAVID ADJAYE

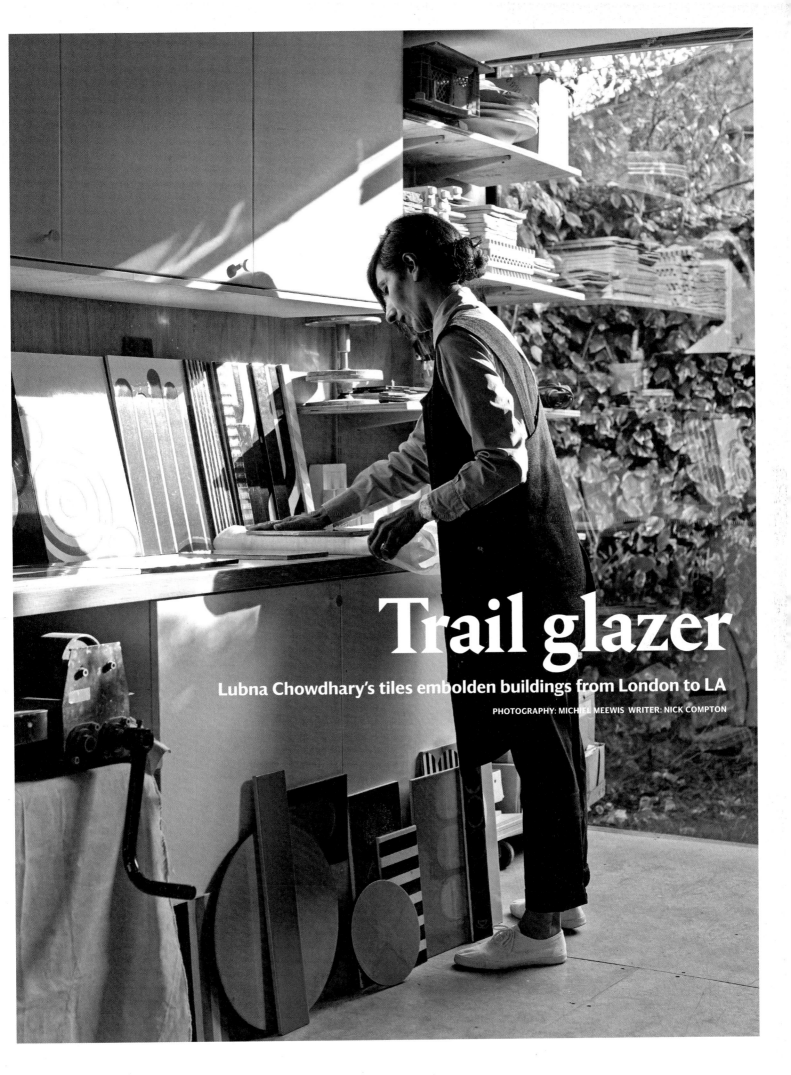

Trail glazer

Lubna Chowdhary's tiles embolden buildings from London to LA

PHOTOGRAPHY: MICHIEL MEEWIS WRITER: NICK COMPTON

Lubna Chowdhary creates ceramic tiles, big and small, square and occasionally round but always of the most remarkable colours, in a David Adjaye-designed workshop at the end of her back garden in Streatham in south London. Her husband, the illustrator Nick Higgins, also works at home, which means they can meet for lunch. It's a nice arrangement.

The pair moved here about ten years ago and immediately thought about building a permanent studio for Chowdhary. 'I'd become tired of places becoming gentrified, of being moved along from the various studios I'd had around London,' she says. 'Everything that's involved in ceramics is heavy – clay, glazes, moulds, kilns – so moving is never easy. I saw an article about a timber-framed house by David Adjaye Associates, so we asked if they'd be interested in doing a small project along similar lines. Much to our surprise, they said yes.' In the studio, essentially a black box with two glass sides, Chowdhary makes tiles for her decorative works and murals, commissioned by the likes of the BBC and Conran + Partners, though she is not averse to using industrial tiles if they fit.

'It really depends on the brief and the surface appropriate to the project,' she says. 'Sometimes the maker's hand needs to be evident and each tile results in something completely unique. Other times, it's much more about precision and geometry and then I'll use a pre-made tile.'

She also mixes her own glazes in the studio, making her remarkable colours. 'Glaze is a material to be respected,' Chowdhary insists. 'It gives a depth of colour and a richness to a surface. It has an integrity. But it's also unpredictable and gives a unique result every time. That's the beauty of it.'

These colours don't exist until after the tiles are fired. 'The colour develops during the firing, so you are always working blind. You have to carry a memory of the colours. The beauty of glaze is that it becomes liquid during the firing and the colours melt into each other when you layer them. I spend a lot of time blending glazes to create new colours. It can be quite addictive.'

The shelves of the studio act as a display for hundreds of her tiles in thousands of shades. Many have contrast circles in the middle. There is a kind of thrumming,

humming dilation to them (though there is a set of more muted tiles on a work table, mounted individually and to be sent to Margaret Howell for sale in Japan. She has also created tiles for the US interiors retailer West Elm, which have developed into a small range of furniture that carries her name).

Chowdhary sequences these tiles into larger compositions until they make a beautiful buzz, like a series of drones. 'I work with the juxtaposition of colours until they bounce off each other, creating an amazing energy,' she says.

One of the shelves in Chowdhary's studio, though, is covered not with tiles but with a small cluster of dun-coloured fantasy modernist buildings in miniature. The little ceramic buildings belong to what you might call Act I of Chowdhary's career. She was

'I was seduced by the immediacy of clay, it needed no tools'

born to Pakistani parents in Tanzania in 1964, but the family moved to Rochdale in the north of England in 1970. Her mother was a seamstress and, with her father, ran a business selling clothes.

After school, Chowdhary studied 3D design at Manchester Metropolitan University. She says that initially she had no interest in ceramics. 'I saw it as a crafty, feminine pursuit. The sort of thing I was trying to distance myself from.' Slowly, though, she began to see the possibilities of the material and the form. 'I was hoping to pursue furniture-making, but one of the compulsory materials on the course was ceramics and I became seduced by its immediacy. It was a material that could be formed without the use of machinery or tools; it responded directly to your hands.'

Chowdhary then moved on to the Royal College of Art in London to study ceramics, where she was taught by the sculptor and artist Eduardo Paolozzi. 'He was very sympathetic and supportive, and I was awarded his travel scholarship and travelled »

SOME OF CHOWDHARY'S DESIGN
NOTES AND FINISHED TILES,
WHICH CAN BE SEEN IN LOCATIONS
FROM A LOS ANGELES BAKERY TO A
POOLSIDE HOTEL BAR IN DELHI AND
A BELGRAVIA ICE CREAM PARLOUR

to South India. Being at the RCA, and in London particularly, really opened up my mind to so many new ideas. I was like a sponge soaking it up, and in the end I just let my hands sort out the influences.

'I started working with clay again and the end result was *Metropolis*, 1,000 objects that sat somewhere between a museum collection and a cityscape.' The mini modernist fantasies are part of this collection. 'I'm interested in architecture from a sculptural and emotional perspective,' says Chowdhary. 'Or as a collection of objects in a city, an environment that contains energy.'

This began almost a decade of gallery shows for Chowdhary, and in 2001 she was shortlisted for the Jerwood Applied Arts prize. It proved a turning point, but not in the direction you might imagine. 'I wanted to do more than make objects that sat on plinths,' she says. 'I wanted to make work that could exist outside the gallery environment.'

Chowdhary was going to address her interest in architecture in a far more direct way. 'I wanted to make work that was integrated with architecture. This way the work becomes part of people's daily life and part of their memory of a place.'

She cites the work Miró did with the ceramicist Josep Llorens Artigas as an influence, particularly their giant mural at Barcelona airport. She is also an admirer of the Brazilian artist and Niemeyer collaborator Athos Bulcão, and the Polish émigré Adam Kossowski, who produced the massive History of the Old Kent Road mural at the former North Peckham Civic Centre in south London.

Chowdhary started making tiles, looking at the way they could work within a space. And learning to work a dimension down. 'In many ways the two-dimensionality of tiles freed me up to explore colour and pattern in a much more focused way. I had one less dimension to think about.'

Her first commissions were from restaurants. 'One was from Terence Conran for Alcazar, a restaurant in Paris. We just cheekily wrote to him asking for a commission and he invited us. It was a completely open brief – almost no brief. I worked on it with my friend, the illustrator Ian Bilbey. It was liberating but also slightly unnerving. The next one was for the first Itsu restaurant, in London's Brompton Cross, before it became a chain. This was completely prescriptive, from the colour palette and the dimensions to the layout.'

The work then started to flow, from public commissions in the UK to work on private interiors in California. You can see Chowdhary's tiles in a bakery in Los Angeles, on café tables in Starkville, Mississippi, behind the poolside bar at The Park Hotel in Delhi and at the Olivogelo gelateria in London's Belgravia. Her work is in a park in Cambridge, a road-side tower in Slough and a housing estate in Haringey. Sometimes the works make up distinct strips, sometimes they take over whole walls, bending around corners.

Increasingly, though, Chowdhary wants to involve herself in architectural projects at an earlier stage, to make her work integral to the design of the building. She has been talking to London-based Makespace architects about collaborating on two new mosques, but admits that client conservatism is a problem. She says that she dreams of one day building an architectural folly, bringing her back to modernist fantasies of *Metropolis* perhaps.

For now, though, there is a lot to be done with her tiles. At the moment she is using bigger tiles: bolder, with a louder thrum, and making greater claims on a space. ★
lubnachowdhary.co.uk

exprimo®

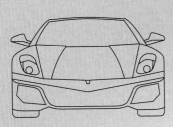

Sports cars of Italy

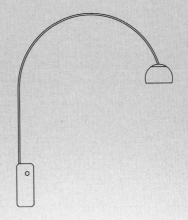

Design of Italy

Fashion of Italy

Ceramics of Italy

THE MARK OF **CERAMIC EXCELLENCE** WORLDWIDE.

Used exclusively by the leading Italian producers of ceramic floor and wall tiles, sanitaryware and tableware, the Ceramics of Italy trademark guarantees unique Italian quality and design. Building professionals, designers and consumers across the world should insist on products bearing the Ceramics of Italy logo – an unquestionable mark of excellence.

Follow us on

www.laceramicaitaliana.it

Ceramics of Italy is a trademark of Confindustria Ceramica - the Italian Association of Ceramics - and Edi.Cer, the organizer of Cersaie, the world's largest international exhibition of ceramic tile and bathroom furnishings (Bologna, Italy - September 22-26, 2014) - www.cersaie.it.

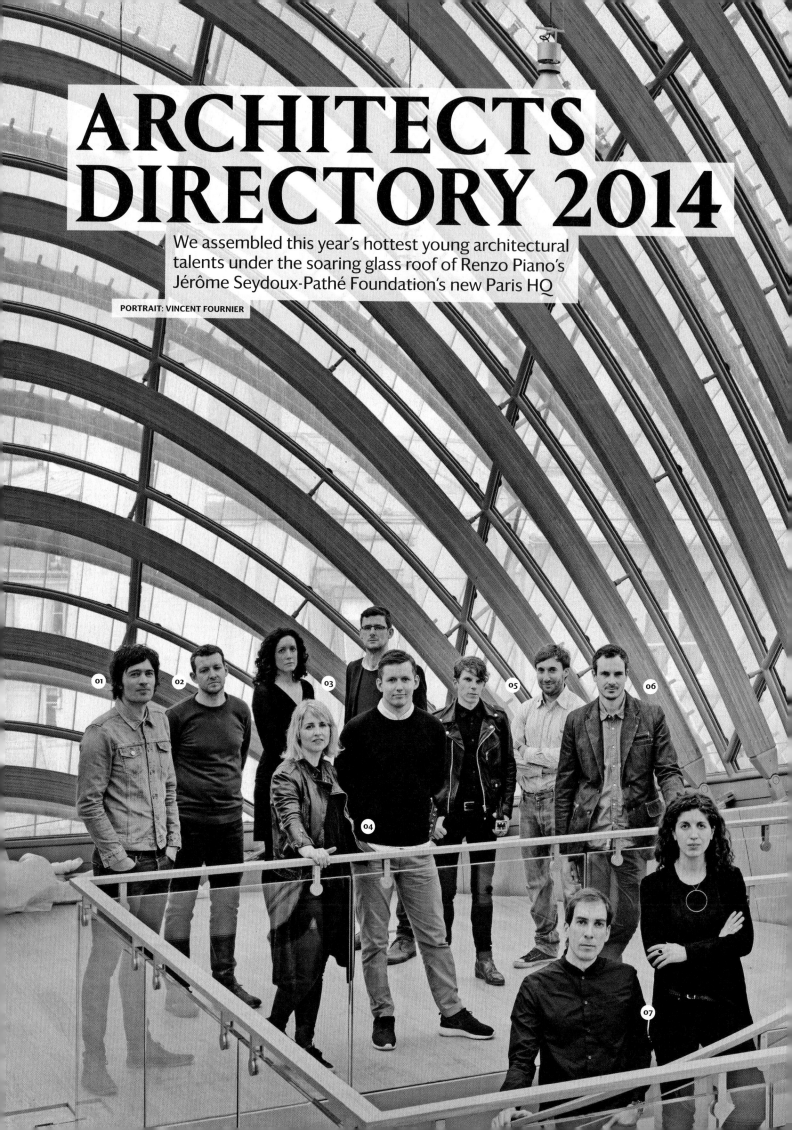

ARCHITECTS DIRECTORY 2014

We assembled this year's hottest young architectural talents under the soaring glass roof of Renzo Piano's Jérôme Seydoux-Pathé Foundation's new Paris HQ

PORTRAIT: VINCENT FOURNIER

OUR GROUP OF ARCHITECTURAL
HIGH FLYERS. FOR DETAILS OF
WHO'S WHO, TURN THE PAGE

Architects Directory

ABOVE, THIS MONTH'S LIMITED-EDITION
COVER (AVAILABLE TO SUBSCRIBERS,
SEE WALLPAPER.COM) BY RENZO PIANO

LEFT, WHEN COMPLETE, THE REAR
OF THE JÉRÔME SEYDOUX-PATHÉ
FOUNDATION HQ WILL FEATURE
A TRANQUIL COURTYARD GARDEN

BELOW, OUR PHOTOGRAPHED
ARCHITECTS (SEE PREVIOUS PAGE)

01	**GRAEME LAUGHLAN**	RAW ARCHITECTURE WORKSHOP, UK
02	**DONALD MATHESON**	MATHESON WHITELEY, UK
03	**KATHRYN WILSON & SHANE COTTER**	ARCHITECTURAL FARM, IRELAND
04	**JOHANNE BORTHNE & VILHELM CHRISTENSEN**	SUPERUNION, NORWAY
05	**SYLVAIN DUBAIL & DAVID BEGERT**	DUBAIL BEGERT, SWITZERLAND
06	**LOÏC PICQUET**	FRANCE
07	**LEONIDAS TRAMPOUKIS & ELENI PETALOTI**	LoT, GREECE
08	**JOSEP CAMPS & OLGA FELIP,**	SPAIN
09	**ERHARD AN-HE KINZELBACH**	KNOWSPACE, GERMANY
10	**SIMON STOREY**	ANONYMOUS, US
11	**OMAR GANDHI,**	CANADA
12	**WENDY EVANS JOSEPH & CHRIS COOPER**	COOPER JOSEPH, US

Passers-by on the Avenue des Gobelins in Paris' 13th arrondissement may notice an organic-shaped 'creature' peeking above the Auguste Rodin sculptures on the façade of No 73. Snuggled within an old city block, its rounded body is covered in aluminium scales reflecting the grey colour of Parisian rooftops. A grey roof was one thing that Sophie Seydoux, president of the Jérôme Seydoux-Pathé Foundation, insisted upon when discussing the design of the Foundation's new headquarters with its architect, Renzo Piano.

Impressed by Piano's 2006 Morgan Library extension in Manhattan, Jérôme and Sophie Seydoux went directly to the Italian architect for the Foundation's new home, to be housed in a former theatre, first built in 1869. This later became one of Paris' first cinemas in the early 1900s, making it a perfect match for Pathé, a cinematographic legend born in 1896 and still a major player in the film industry.

The newly sited Foundation will open in September. Researchers will occupy the two upper levels, generously lit through the glass dome and clad in a warm, all-wood interior, while screening and exhibition rooms will be housed on the lower floors. There are plans to organise workshops for children to discover the materiality of movie making. Pathé's vast archives will be sandwiched in the two floors in-between, at the building's heart.

Having the entire construction process pass through the existing building's 5m-wide listed façade was among the project's major challenges. Architect Thorsten Sahlmann, who worked on both the Morgan Library and the Foundation, explains that the building's new glass entrance facilitates the transition between the historic frontage and 'the creature'. The project's reduced footprint (the original theatre covered a larger volume) offers additional breathing space for the neighbours and a courtyard garden, while the glass dome improves natural lighting in the adjacent apartment blocks.

For our 2014 Architects Directory photo shoot, we gathered some of the world's best emerging architects under this breathtaking glass dome and, over the page, we profile the 12 photographed practices (a further eight studio profiles can be found online) with the aid of computer-generated imagery created by artist Richard Kolker.
rpbw.com, fondation-jeromeseydoux-pathe.com

PHOTOGRAPHY: MICHEL DENANCÉ   WRITER: ANNA YUDINA

Wallpaper*
City Guide

LONDON

PHAIDON

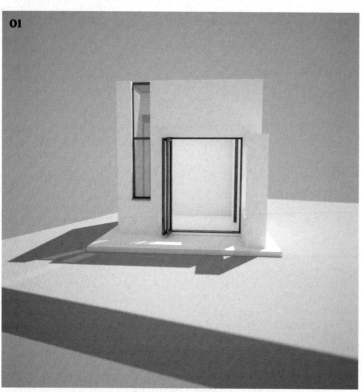

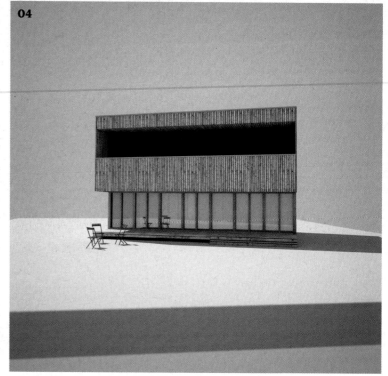

01. ARCHITECTURAL FARM
Ireland

Shane Cotter and Kathryn Wilson set up their practice in their home town of Dublin in 2010. Their Blackpitts project was key to the practice's development, and other work includes the refurbishment and extension of a house in Milltown, Dublin (pictured). The pair have also used their love of drawing to introduce school children to architecture by participating in workshops, which subsequently developed into the local DRAW programme.
www.architecturalfarm.com

02. MATHESON WHITELEY
UK

Prior to opening their firm in 2012, Donald Matheson was a project leader for Tony Fretton before working on Tate Modern's Tanks project, while Jason Whiteley spent six years at Herzog & de Meuron. A substantial amount of their workload is residential and in the arts, building galleries and studios for the likes of Martino Gamper and Max Lamb (pictured). Upcoming projects include a major media company fit-out in London's Sea Containers House.
www.mathesonwhiteley.com

03. DUBAIL BEGERT
Switzerland

Establishing their firm just three years after graduating from EPFL, David Begert and Sylvain Dubail have always had a hands-on approach to creating buildings that are affordable, functional and strive to elevate the ordinary in some special way. Some of their most recent projects include a Jura tourist office and the renovation and improved thermal efficiency of a two-storey 1970s house in Saignelégier (pictured), in north-west Switzerland.
www.dbarch.ch

04. LOÏC PICQUET
France

French architect Loïc Picquet set up his practice in Altkirch, near the Swiss and German borders, in 2012. The architect focuses his designs around three important elements: responding to a building's needs according to its locale and history, working with an open plan, and choosing the right materials. Recent work includes the Maison L (pictured), a minimalist, two-level house made of larch wood sited on a hill in the architect's home town.
www.picquet-architecte.com

ARTWORK: RICHARD KOLKER WRITERS: JONATHAN BELL AND ELLIE STATHAKI

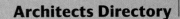

For more practice
profiles and images,
go to Wallpaper.com

**05. RAW ARCHITECTURE
WORKSHOP, UK**
After six years at Foster and
Partners, Graeme Laughlan
set up his London practice,
completing his first new build,
the House at Camusdarach Sands
(pictured), last year. A stunningly
bold structure, clad in black-
stained wood, the house's bright
interior is a stark contrast. Citing
a wide range of influences, from
Bobby Gillespie to Gillespie, Kidd
& Coia, other projects include his
Modular temporary bar solution.
rawarchitectureworkshop.com

06. ANONYMOUS
US

New Zealand-born Simon Storey's LA practice combines a love of classic SoCal modernism with the desire to build without reusing familiar styles. Faced with plenty of steep lots in the Californian canyons, it has ample opportunity to work with light and structure. Storey describes the firm's recent Big & Small House (pictured) as 'a wonderful balance between a tiny budget and a grand living space', but his ultimate ambition is an innovative skyscraper.
www.anonymousarchitects.com

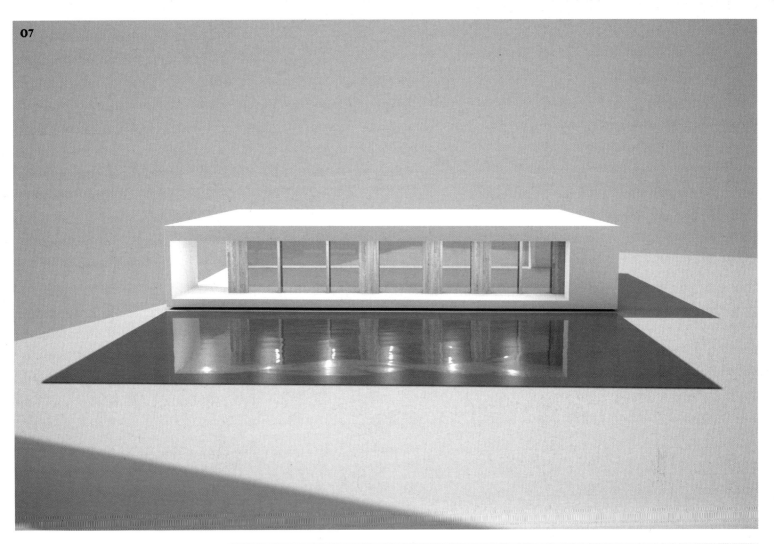

07. JOSEP CAMPS OLGA FELIP ARQUITECTURA
Spain

Spanish duo Olga Felip and Josep Camps founded their firm in 2006, looking to reinvent traditional Catalan culture in a contemporary way. Their civic work includes the elegantly austere health centre in L'Aldea and the Ferreries Cultural Centre, a sober structure that contrasts its dark exterior with a symphony in striated light within, while residential projects include the sleek, single-storey Villa Sifera (pictured).
www.josepcampsolgafelip.net

08. COOPER JOSEPH
US

Prior to setting up in New York in 2008, Chris Cooper was at SOM, while Wendy Evans Joseph was with Pei Cobb Freed. Many of the firm's projects exist at the intersection of architecture and art, such as 'Starlight', a light installation made from thousands of floating LED chips. The Writer's Studio (pictured) in upstate NY is a sublime piece of functional sculpture, while the Webb Chapel Park Pavilion in Texas resonates with a rich yellow interior.
www.cooperjosephstudio.com

08

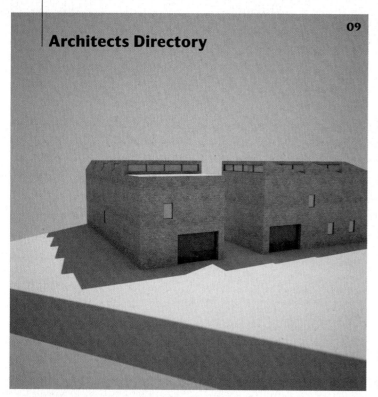

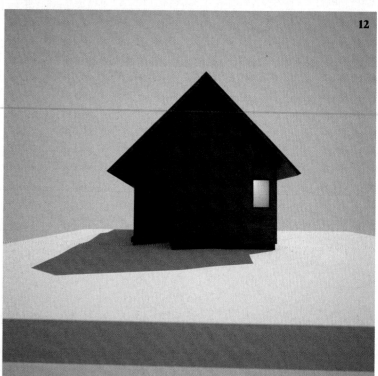

09. KNOWSPACE
Germany

Knowspace, says Erhard An-He Kinzelbach, 'was founded in New York, matured in Vienna and Hangzhou and currently operates from Berlin'. Its portfolio includes twin studio houses for two artists in Songzhuang (pictured) and a courthouse building in St Pölten. Each project's conflicts are a big part of what drives Kinzelbach's design process, as do the architect's mentors, who over the years have included Farshid Moussavi and Wang Shu.
www.knowspace.eu

10. SUPERUNION
Norway

Vilhelm Christensen and Johanne Borthne's Oslo practice has a multidisciplinary approach that has won them a nomination for Norsk Form's Prize for Young Architects, and the opportunity to design for Norway's acclaimed National Tourist Routes project. Recent works include a house extension in the Ekeberg hills (pictured). Plus, their proposal for a Disaster Prevention Centre in Istanbul piqued the interest of rapper Kanye West.
www.superunion.no

11. LoT
Greece

Founded in 2011 by the Columbia University-trained Leonidas Trampoukis and Eleni Petaloti, LoT is about to complete one of its biggest residential projects to date, the Cubic Housing (pictured) in Thessaloniki, which has been welcomed as the best project of the year by the local architecture press. Different materials, light and colour patterns are all part of the office's pool of inspiration, contributing to its growing cross-disciplinary portfolio.
lot-arch.com

12. OMAR GANDHI
Canada

The architecture office of Halifax-based Omar Gandhi may be young - founded only four years ago - yet its design skills and confidence speak volumes. The Moore Studio in Hubbards, Nova Scotia, sits among Gandhi's favourite projects, but he has worked on a number of beautifully designed single-family houses - both main homes and holiday retreats, including the Black Gables live/work studio (pictured) in Cape Breton, Nova Scotia.
omargandhi.com

FUTURE CAPITAL

13-30 June

The exhibition 'Future Capital: The 2014 Wallpaper* Architects Directory' (for venue, see Wallpaper.com) will present this year's architect selection through artwork by Richard Kolker and feature a bespoke ceramic installation in association with Ceramics of Italy. The show is part of the London Festival of Architecture.

Also featuring

The exhibition will include eight more practices, including BXB Studio, whose Artist's House is pictured below. For a profile of the studio, plus the seven other practices (Salad, Sundaymorning, Rizoma Arquitetura, Haberstroh Architekten, Arquitectos Matos, A-CH, and HLPS Arquitectos), visit Wallpaper.com

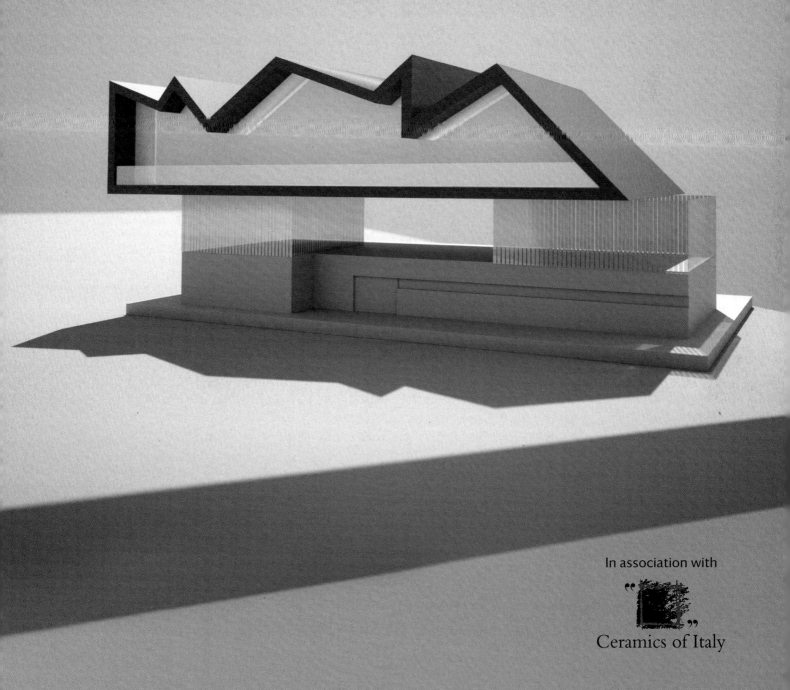

In association with

Ceramics of Italy

Valentina Algeri for Cersaie 2014
Civica Scuola Arte & Messaggio Milan - Visual Design

ARMANDO TESTA

CERSAIE
BOLOGNA ▪ ITALY
INTERNATIONAL EXHIBITION
OF CERAMIC TILE AND BATHROOM
FURNISHINGS

22-26 SEPTEMBER 2014
www.cersaie.it

Organized by **EDI.CER. spa**   Promoted by **CONFINDUSTRIA CERAMICA**   In collaboration with 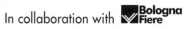 **Bologna Fiere**

Show Management: PROMOS srl - P.O. Box 37 - 40050 CENTERGROSS BOLOGNA (Italy) - Tel. +39.051.6646000 - Fax +39.051.862514
Press Office: EDI.CER. spa - Viale Monte Santo 40 - 41049 SASSUOLO MO (Italy) - Tel. +39.0536.804585 - Fax +39.0536.806510

Advertising Campaign co-financed by   *Ministero dello Sviluppo Economico*

TAKESHI YAMANAKA,
PRESIDENT OF MARUNI,
IN THE COMPANY FACTORY
ON A 'HIROSHIMA'
CHAIR DESIGNED BY
NAOTO FUKASAWA

1928
Showa Bentwood Factory
founded in Hiroshima

1933
The company is rebranded
as Maruni

1968
Launch of the highly
successful Classic line

2004
First collaboration with
international designers,
operating under the
Nextmaruni banner

2008
Naoto Fukasawa's
Hiroshima series launched

2014
New furniture by Naoto
Fukasawa and Jasper
Morrison presented at
Salone del Mobile in Milan.
Maruni furniture sold in
25 countries worldwide

Wood working

The industrialised craft of Japanese furniture maker Maruni matches man and machine

About an hour from Hiroshima's city centre, in a lush, picture-postcard location, lies one of Japan's oldest furniture manufacturers. Founded in 1928 as the Showa Bentwood Factory, the company (now named Maruni Wood Industry) is still being true to founder Takeo Yamanaka's mission to 'industrialise craft'.

Until the present company president, Takeshi Yamanaka, took over the family company in 2001 (the company founder was his grandfather's brother), Maruni was mainly known for making highly decorative and fussy, glossy-finished furniture. His first thought was that the company wasn't making

any furniture he would buy himself. There was a large catalogue of ornamental, European-inspired furniture but nothing that fitted a more modern, simple lifestyle. The production process was highly automated with the decorative carvings and parts being made by CNC routers and milling machines. This meant consistent quality and uniformity, as well as keeping the cost of the product at reasonable levels, but Yamanaka felt the design aspect was missing, something unique that only a Japanese manufacturer like Maruni could deliver.

The first thing Yamanaka did was to close Maruni's overseas factories in China and Thailand.»

THE PRODUCTION OF THE 'HIROSHIMA' CHAIR IS A MARRIAGE BETWEEN MACHINE MANUFACTURE AND MANUAL CRAFTSMANSHIP. NAOTO FUKASAWA INSISTS THE TWO ARMRESTS ARE CUT FROM THE SAME PIECE OF BEECH

FOR MORE IMAGES FROM THE MARUNI PRODUCTION HUB, DOWNLOAD THE IPAD EDITION AT WALLPAPER.COM/IPAD

first product proposal was the 'Hiroshima' chair. After a lot of trial and error, and weeks of programming the various CNC milling machines, production is now running at a smooth 400 chairs a month. While much of the process is done by machines, the initial wood selection, assembly of the 12 parts that make up the chair, and finishing is done by hand. Fukasawa is a perfectionist and specifies that the two armrests are cut of the same piece of beech, guaranteeing a matching finish. He is also, since 2010, acting as Maruni's creative director, overseeing all new designs that leave the factory floor.

Yamanaka feels very strongly about keeping production within Japan. 'This country is not normally seen as a furniture producer, because of our tradition of sitting on tatami mats on the floor,' he explains. 'But in terms of carpentry and working with wood, Japan has a long and highly developed tradition.' Combine this love affair with wood and craftsmanship with Toyota-style production management and hi-tech manufacturing robots and you understand Maruni's success.

'Our Japanese craftsmen have a special sensibility and attention to detail. They will polish the underside of tables and chairs even if these are not visible to the end consumers.' And this perfectionism shows.

Newly launched and updated pieces designed by Naoto Fukasawa and Jasper Morrison are the latest additions to the Maruni collection. Fukasawa's 'Roundish' sofa is an extension of his earlier chair and is finished with cobalt fabric from Kvadrat. Morrison, who has been designing for Maruni regularly since 2011, has added a pale ash version of the 'Lightwood' chair with a mesh seat, and the inviting new 'Bruno' sofa.

The products are shipped abroad in larger and larger numbers, to more than 25 countries around the globe. There is a wall in the factory where Yamanaka likes to put up prints of the latest international projects that are using Maruni products – not to show off, but to boost the confidence and morale of the hundred or so people working on the floor.

The hope is that about a third of the production will eventually be sold overseas. Meanwhile, monthly shipping to a recently opened European warehouse will help to reduce lead time and bring Maruni's touch-perfect products to cafés, restaurants, and dining and living rooms around the globe. ✱
www.maruni.com

'My predecessors had been focusing on cost and high turnover, but I felt we had to go in a completely new direction,' he explains. Yamanaka consulted architect and product designer Masayuki Kurokawa and they decided to ask 12 international designers to create pieces 'born from the Japanese aesthetic', which were first presented in Milan at Salone del Mobile in 2005 under the Nextmaruni heading. 'I told the craftsmen at the factory that they should make the furniture exactly as the designers drew it,' says Yamanaka. He wanted to learn and hoped that his co-workers on the factory floor would absorb new ideas and techniques too.

The press and Salone visitors alike loved the completely new and light chairs of the Nextmaruni collection. Participation by world-renowned designers such as Alberto Meda, SANAA, Naoto Fukasawa and Jasper Morrison also helped to draw a crowd, but despite all the attention, Maruni failed to capitalise on the production of the designs.

In early 2007, Yamanaka, hat in hand, visited Naoto Fukasawa. 'We were almost broke and couldn't really offer Fukasawa any guarantees, but everyone I had spoken to, including the craftsmen at our factory, was recommending that we should go to Fukasawa as he really seemed to understand our company.' Fukasawa's

Molteni & C

Gliss Walk-In wardrobe – Nature bed Ferruccio Laviani **D.950.1 framed mirrors** Gio Ponti

PERFECTLY SUITED

Tailoring fabric on the furnishings and a lamp that's
a shirt. Why Brioni and Michael Anastassiades
joined forces to create this year's best dressed room

PHOTOGRAPHY: PHILIP SINDEN WRITER: ROSA BERTOLI

If Wallpaper* Handmade were an academy, we'd like to think of Brioni and Michael Anastassiades as two of our most notable alumni. Over the last five years, both have lent their vision and expertise multiple times to our annual celebration of design and craftsmanship, helping to create unique products to be exhibited in Milan during Salone del Mobile, and showcased in Wallpaper's August issue.

Greek-born, London-based designer Anastassiades has reproduced a Jaipur street barber's hut with Studio Mumbai (W*149), and created impossibly curved marble 'Miracle Chips' with Tuscan marble producer Henraux (W*173). Brioni, meanwhile, hosted the Handmade exhibition in its Milanese

palazzo, on via Gesù, for three years. It also collaborated with architects Carmody Groarke on an installation based on the 12,000 stitches of a Brioni suit jacket (W*137); with designer Konstantin Grcic on a cape inspired by the brand's archive (W*149); and with Dutch artists Lernert & Sander, who outfitted a hand with a suit (W*161).

This year, we brought together these two Handmade stalwarts in another Wallpaper* first. 'I have been an admirer of Michael's work for a long time,' says Brioni creative director Brendan Mullane. 'I thought how great the simplicity and purity in his crafted work was, and that it would be amazing to do something with him for Brioni.' In April, the two joined forces to work on a project that

was previewed with a teaser in Wallpaper* Handmade's debut off-site installation during Milan's Salone del Mobile. Anastassiades and Mullane upholstered three windows of the Brioni palazzo with the brand's suit fabrics, alongside a display of the designer's lighting. Now, their collaboration is about to come to completion, with an installation to mark the opening of Brioni's new boutique, a 1,200 sq m space within the palazzo.

'I was interested in finding common ground,' says Anastassiades when describing the initial stages of his planning for the installation. 'I realised that Brioni and I share many values, and one is definitely quality – quality of making, quality of materials – but also an appreciation of the way things are »

MICHAEL ANASTASSIADES
AT BRIONI'S TAILORING
WORKSHOP IN PENNE, TRYING
AN UNFINISHED JACKET FOR SIZE

OPPOSITE, A MODEL OF THE
INSTALLATION HE HAS CREATED
WITH BRENDAN MULLANE,
A ROOM SET AND FURNISHINGS
UPHOLSTERED IN BRIONI FABRICS

Design

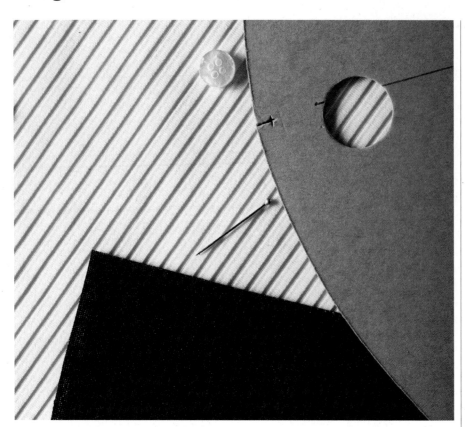

LEFT, DETAILS FROM THE
SHIRT-MAKING PROCESS AT
THE BRIONI FACTORY

01. THE INSTALLATION
COMPRISES A BOX MADE UP
OF UPHOLSTERED PANELS,
FEATURING FOUR SHEETS
OF BRIONI SUITING FABRIC
ON EACH SIDE.

02. THE PANELS WILL BE 5CM
THICK, IN TIMBER OR ALUMINIUM,
AND ARE DESIGNED TO BE EASILY
DISMANTLED AND REASSEMBLED

03. THE FINISHED STRUCTURE,
2.7M WIDE AND DEEP, AND 3.2M
HIGH, WILL HOUSE THE
UPHOLSTERED FURNISHINGS
AND SHIRT-FABRIC LAMP

ILLUSTRATOR: EOIN RYAN

made, and the skills that go into making something of a simple nature.'

Anastassiades had a brief glimpse of the fashion world when he designed Hussein Chalayan's fashion show sets in the late 1990s, but hasn't worked in fashion since. 'I find it interesting, the idea of me as a designer coming into the world of fashion, exploring its different techniques and materials; I like to submerge myself in a different world.'

For this project, design and tailoring met half way, and Anastassiades' ideas developed into a room inspired by the layers that go into a suit, and the intricate stitching that holds everything together. The installation is a box, whose walls, ceiling and floor are lined with dark suiting fabric, furnished with two chairs and a table dressed in the same material, with a lamp made of crisp white shirt fabric hanging above. 'It's a rather archetypical scenario,' Anastassiades explains. 'Archetype of a table, archetype of a chair, and a light.'

The collaboration has a serendipitous feel. Both Anastassiades and Mullane are humble souls with a perfectionist attitude to their work. 'Michael has a passion for materials, something I am also obsessive about,' says Mullane when describing the synergies that brought the two together. 'I can see we both have a real appreciation of the beauty in how things are constructed. In our work there is a sense of control that leads to things being expressed and created in a pure form, the working process is full of details and finishing that are almost invisible to the human eye, but we know they are there.'

Hidden detail is at the core of the installation, where the lighting lends a sense

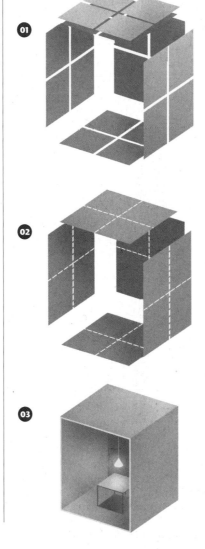

of discovery. Anastassiades developed his shirt-fabric lamp as a cone with a dark base, so that the light, instead of being directed downwards, is cast outwards into the room as a soft glow through the translucent shirt material. Entering the dim space, he explains, the viewer doesn't immediately see the details, as the materials absorb all the light. 'As your eyes adjust to the light, slowly you start discovering more.' Details such as the stitching, the simplicity of the visual language and the archetypical shapes come to life. 'As a concept, this reflects the common language that Brioni and I share,' he adds, describing the installation as 'a suit for furniture and a shirt lamp'.

A triumph of craftsmanship and precision, the installation is being hand-assembled and retouched by the Brioni team, headed by master tailor Angelo Petrucci, under the close supervision of Mullane and Anastassiades. 'Our tailors are fantastic and really rise to the challenge of working on a project like this with such passion and skill,' notes Mullane, adding that 'handmade to me means something made with a human touch, thinking and feeling'.

To be unveiled on 21 June, when the new Brioni boutique opens, the installation sees the passion and craft of Anastassiades and Mullane collide in the perfect joint expression of their aesthetics. Which is very much the essence of Wallpaper* Handmade: bringing diverse strengths together to create the extraordinary.
Brioni, via Gesù 2A, Milan, www.brioni.com, michaelanastassiades.com. You can see this year's Wallpaper Handmade projects in the August issue, on sale 10 July*

KETTAL

outdoor furniture

A tribute to light

artemide.com

Jean Nouvel: Objective

Artemide®

CLOCKWISE FROM TOP LEFT, 'ODA' LIGHT, €1,490, BY SEBASTIAN HERKNER, FOR PULPO. 'ASTON' SOFA, £4,950, BY RODOLFO DORDONI, FOR MINOTTI. 'LEGNO BASE' OAK FLOORING, €130 PER SQ M, BY BOEN, FOR BRIX. 'PIUMA' LOW TABLE, FROM £8,426, BY ANTONIO CITTERIO, FOR FLEXFORM. PITCHER, £305; DECANTER, £270; GLASSES, £135 EACH, ALL BY BOTTEGA VENETA. 'IPANEMA' ARMCHAIRS, FROM €2,623 EACH, BY JEAN-MARIE MASSAUD, FOR POLIFORM. 'ORGANIQUE' LOW TABLE, FROM €1,135, BY DRAGA & AUREL, FOR BAXTER

FOR STOCKISTS, SEE PAGE 224

LIVING ROOM

Welcome to the W* House, domestic space's final frontier

PHOTOGRAPHY: LEONARDO SCOTTI INTERIORS: AMY HEFFERNAN

■ 'WING' SOFA
by Antonio Citterio

Antonio Citterio and Flexform celebrated their prolific 40-year collaboration with a new selection of pieces that cover all furnishing bases, from tables and seating systems to lamps. With a lightness of form that's enhanced by its modular shape and a low, detached back, the 'Wing' sofa is classic Citterio. Two discreet metal legs ensure the seat appears to float, cloud-like, in the living space. *'Wing' sofa, £7,397, by Antonio Citterio, for Flexform, www.flexform.it*

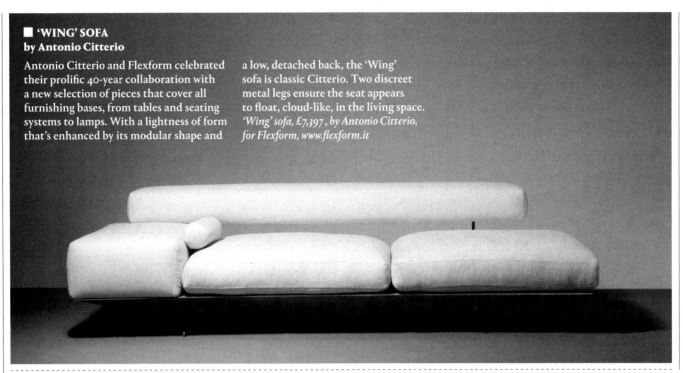

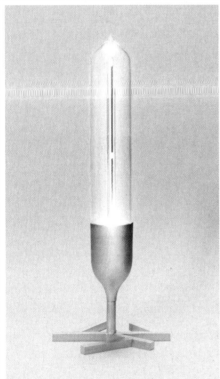

◀ 'EDI' TABLE LAMP
by Alberto Biagetti

Milan-based Alberto Biagetti's 'Edi' series of lamps is inspired by Thomas Edison's most revolutionary invention. In a quest to reimagine the light bulb, he and Venini's expert glassmakers produced this elongated, polychromatic version on a brass base. *'Edi' light, €1,650, by Alberto Biagetti, for Venini, www.venini.com*

▶ 'CONTRORA' ARMCHAIR
by Ron Gilad

Controra is a southern Italian notion that indicates the early hours of the afternoon, traditionally dedicated to resting. The word was aptly chosen to name Ron Gilad's new seating collection, where a generous velvet seat overflows from a rigid wooden frame. *'Controra' armchair, €3,310, by Ron Gilad, for Molteni & C, www.molteni.it*

▶ 'FAGIOLO' TABLE
by Roberto Lazzeroni

Roberto Lazzeroni's study of symmetry and asymmetry in wooden structures has been at the centre of his work for Ceccotti Collezioni since the 1990s. His latest piece, the 'Fagiolo' table, is a minimal addition to this project. Available in a variety of colours and finishes, the small double-decker table is made of a solid American walnut frame holding two bean-shaped tops in marble and glass – *fagiolo* being the Italian word for bean. *'Fagiolo' table, from €1,980, by Roberto Lazzeroni, for Ceccotti Collezioni, www.ceccotticollezioni.it*

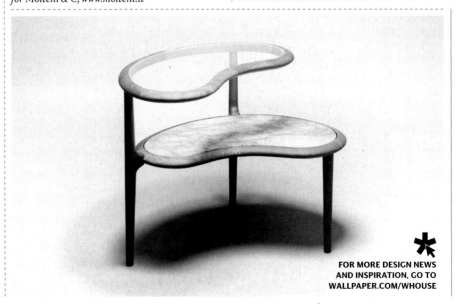

*
**FOR MORE DESIGN NEWS
AND INSPIRATION, GO TO
WALLPAPER.COM/WHOUSE**

THE SOFA & CHAIR COMPANY

LONDON

Handcrafted Heritage
QUALITY FURNITURE MADE IN BRITAIN

CLOCKWISE FROM TOP LEFT, 'THE ANALOG' CLOCK, PRICE ON REQUEST, BY SHANE SCHNECK, FOR HAY. 'ABALLS' HANGING LAMP, €795, BY JAIME HAYON, FOR PARACHILNA. 'SINE' CLOTHES RACK, €500, BY STUDIO EO. 'EOS' TROLLEY TABLE, PRICE ON REQUEST, BY CHI WING LO, FOR GIORGETTI. 'TITUS' VASES, PART OF THE NEW ROMAN COLLECTION, FROM £450, BY JAIME HAYON, FOR PAOLA C. 'ROMBOO' WALL FINISH, FROM €230 PER SQ M, BY SALVATORI. 'HOLD ON' DAYBED, €2,404, BY NICOLA GALLIZIA, FOR THONET. 'BRUSHSTROKE' CONSOLE, £1,533, BY NENDO, FOR GLAS ITALIA

FOR STOCKISTS, SEE PAGE 224

HALLWAY

Where good first impressions count

PHOTOGRAPHY: LEONARDO SCOTTI INTERIORS: AMY HEFFERNAN

▲ 'PINORAMA' WALL-MOUNTED PINBOARD
by Inga Sempé

Inga Sempé's first collaboration with Hay is the perfect addition to the Danish company's elegant, well-priced collection. The Parisian designer's wall-hanging panels are made of a brick-patterned metal grid that can be equipped with shelves, mirrors, hooks and cylindrical pots to hold small items. The structure is backed with a cork panel to which you can pin cards and papers.
'Pinorama' wall-mounted pinboard, price on request, by Inga Sempé, for Hay, www.hay.dk

◄ 'HEMISPHERE' LAMP AND MIRROR
by Olga Bielawska
Olga Bielawska impresses with her playful approach to shapes. From the Bauhaus graduate's latest collection, a mix of delicate furniture and smaller objects, we love this lamp and mirror, each set in a turned oak hemisphere with a small glass stand.
'Hemisphere' lamp and mirror, prices on request, by Olga Bielawska, www.bielawska.de

➔ 'AUDREY' DOOR HANDLE
by Jean-François D'Or

Brussels-based Jean-François D'Or has created a pink gold door handle that plays on the contrast between matte and polished surfaces and reflects the architecture around it. The moniker is a nod to Audrey Hepburn, a name that was always sure to open doors.
'Audrey' door handle, €291, by Jean-François D'Or, for Maison Vervloet, www.vervloet.com

◄ 'ANIN' STOOL
by David Lopez Quincoces

We were drawn to the stark simplicity of David Lopez Quincoces' 'Anin' stool, a piece that confirms the Milan-based Spanish designer's penchant for graphic lines and a pure aesthetic. The stool, his second contribution to Living Divani's collection, following last year's 'Track' sofa, features a basic seat placed atop an X-shaped, powder-coated aluminium structure, which appears two dimensional when seen from the side. A lesson in rigorous geometry.
'Anin' stool, €956, by David Lopez Quincoces, for Living Divani, www.livingdivani.it

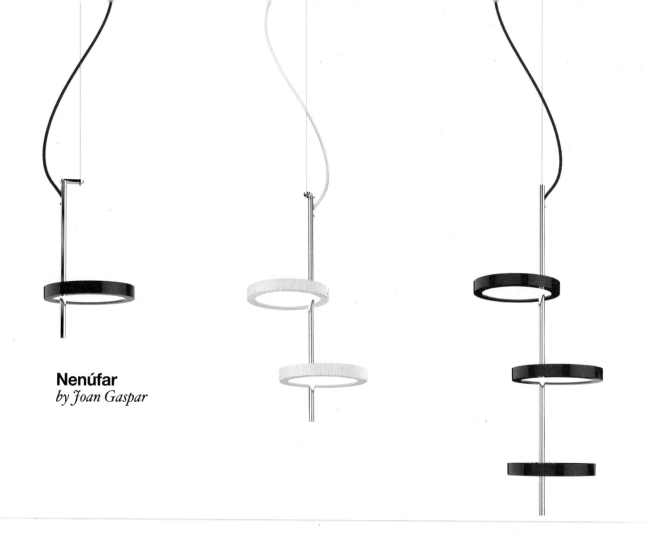

Nenúfar
by Joan Gaspar

Tak*ing care* of l*ight*.

marset
BARCELONA

CLOCKWISE FROM TOP,
'HARP' RECLINING CHAIR,
PRICE ON REQUEST,
BY RODOLFO DORDONI,
FOR RODA. 'PHYTOPHILER'
PLANT POTS, FROM
€450, BY DOSSOFIORITO.
'NIGHTINGALE' LED
LANTERN, FROM €320,
BY CHRISTOPHE DE LA
FONTAINE AND ROSENTHAL,
FOR DANTE GOODS AND
BADS. CORK-LIDDED
CONTAINER TABLE, €252,
BY NAOTO FUKASAWA, FOR
SERRALUNGA. 'KETTAL ROLL'
CHAIR, €1,650, BY PATRICIA
URQUIOLA, FOR KETTAL.
MARBLE TABLES, €2,260,
BY LUDOVICA & ROBERTO
PALOMBA, FOR EXTETA

FOR STOCKISTS, SEE PAGE 224

OUTDOORS

A corking container, hot pots and seating with an outside edge

PHOTOGRAPHY: LEONARDO SCOTTI INTERIORS: AMY HEFFERNAN

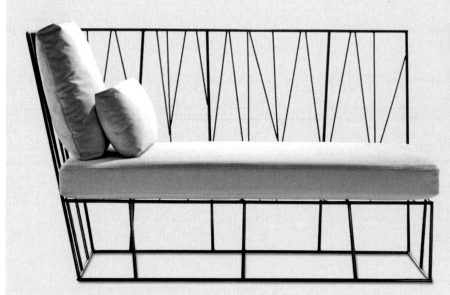

◄ 'HERVÉ' SEAT
by Lievore Altherr Molina

When it comes to outdoor furniture, it's hard to match this for sophisticated elegance. Designed for Driade, Lievore Altherr Molina's five-piece 'Hervé' collection comprises seating and small tables. Combining graphic frames and stark white cushions, the seating's juxtaposition of strong geometry and soft upholstery makes it an enticing addition to our poolside set-up. *'Hervé' seat, £3,222, by Lievore Altherr Molina, for Driade, www.driade.it*

◄ 'BISTRÒ' PARASOL
by Fattorini + Rizzini + Partners

Paola Lenti collections aim to create new domestic landscapes, and this sunshade by Milanese design studio Fattorini + Rizzini + Partners is a playful nod in this direction. The parasol sits on an upholstered pouffe, and is equipped with a detachable side table. *'Bistrò' parasol, €6,528; 'Clique' pouffe, €2,544; 'Clique' table, from €936, all by Fattorini + Rizzini + Partners, for Paola Lenti, www.paolalenti.it*

→ 'AHNDA' CHAIR
by Stephen Burks

Weaving is the focus of US designer Stephen Burks' work, from commissions by major brands to his own 'Man Made' collaboration with Senegalese basket weavers. New for Dedon is his experiment in 'invisible upholstery', this chair covered in a loosely woven net that shows its inner structure. *'Ahnda' chair, price on request, by Stephen Burks, for Dedon, www.dedon.de*

* FOR MORE DESIGN NEWS AND INSPIRATION, GO TO WALLPAPER.COM/WHOUSE

→ 'FACADE' POTS
by Marco Guazzini

Concrete would perhaps not be our first material of choice when sourcing plant pots, but Italian designer Marco Guazzini, who has his studio in Milan, convinced us otherwise with his 'Facade' collection of vases. Inspired by urban skylines, the pots are geometric compositions of pastel-coloured sheets of concrete, whose shapes appear to change depending on the viewing angle and the shadows. Guazzini likes his designs to evoke emotions in the user. These vases make us so content, we're finding a place for them indoors too (see page 115). *'Facade' pots, €238, by Marco Guazzini, marcoguazzini.com*

PHOTOGRAPHY: DANIELE DE CAROLIS WRITER: ROSA BERTOLI

nya nordiska

creative
concept

nanimarquina

Rabari

Design by **Doshi Levien**

Nipa Doshi

Interiors from Spain

Head Office
Església 10, 3er D
08024 Barcelona (Spain)
T + 34 932 376 465
F + 34 932 175 774
info@nanimarquina.com
www.nanimarquina.com

Shop
Rosselló 256/Av. Diagonal
08037 Barcelona (Spain)
T + 34 934 871 606
F + 34 934 871 574
bcnshop@nanimarquina.com

USA Showroom
588 Broadway, Suite 607
New York, NY 10012 (USA)
T + 1 646 701 7058
usa@nanimarquina.com

Photographer **Albert Font**

CLOCKWISE FROM TOP LEFT, 'DIVINA' CALENDAR, ONE-OFF SHOWPIECE, BY GRAPHIC THOUGHT FACILITY, FOR KVADRAT. 'PERSEPOLIS' DESK, £3,555, PART OF THE METROPOLIS COLLECTION, BY GIACOMO MOOR, FOR MEMPHIS POST DESIGN. ON DESK, DUPLEX FOLDER, €8.50; WOODEN RULER, €7, BOTH BY FABRIANO. 'UNCINO' CHAIR, €819, BY RONAN & ERWAN BOUROULLEC, FOR MATTIAZZI. 'EQUILIBRIST' LAMP, PRICE ON REQUEST, BY JEAN NOUVEL, FOR ARTEMIDE. 'ALMORA' ARMCHAIR, PRICE ON REQUEST, BY DOSHI LEVIEN, FOR B&B ITALIA. 'CANTILEVER' SHELVES, FROM €3,970, BY GIULIANO CAPPELLETTI, FOR DE CASTELLI

FOR STOCKISTS, SEE PAGE 224

STUDY

A capacious chair and a dash of flair gets the job done

PHOTOGRAPHY: LEONARDO SCOTTI INTERIORS: AMY HEFFERNAN

* FOR MORE DESIGN NEWS AND INSPIRATION, GO TO WALLPAPER.COM/WHOUSE

↘ 'PLY' SOCKET
by Christoph Friedrich Wagner

We are intrigued by young German designer Wagner's use of plywood, bringing a new aesthetic to lighting, furniture and small objects. His multiple socket, with a textile cord in a choice of colours, stands out as a simple update of a humble essential.
'Ply' socket, price on request, by Christoph Friedrich Wagner, www.christophfriedrichwagner.com

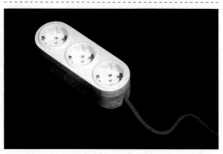

↘ 'PANTOGRAPHE' LAMP
by Michele De Lucchi

Tasked with turning the Hermès philosophy into a lighting collection, Italian architect Michele De Lucchi spent three years on the brand's first lights. The 'Pantographe' is inspired by a draughtsman's instrument, a poetic balancing act of leather and steel.
'Pantographe' lamp, £6,175, by Michele De Lucchi, for Hermès, www.hermes.com

↑ 'TUBO' DESK AND CHAIR
by Sam Hecht and Kim Colin

One for our dream study, this fresh-looking desk and chair set features a combination of marble and plastic set onto steel frames. It was created by the design duo behind Industrial Facility for TOG, a promising brand that debuted at Salone del Mobile this year. Hailing from Brazil, TOG (subtitled 'All Creators Together') presents itself as a platform for dialogue between designers, creators and customers. Its collections are kept simple, with humorous touches and ample scope for customisation.
'Tubo' desk; chair, prices on request, both by Sam Hecht and Kim Colin, for TOG, www.togallcreatorstogether.com

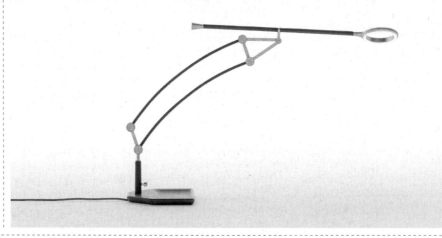

← 'NEAT' DESK ORGANISERS
by Johan van Hengel

Rotterdam-based designer Johan van Hengel is behind a small yet perfectly formed selection of furniture and accessories that combine essential lines with a somewhat nostalgic aesthetic. With our penchant for rigour in the workspace, we were immediately attracted to his aptly named 'Neat' wooden trays, with metal edges of varying heights and colours. These not only partition a desktop (handy when you're working in a communal space) but also hold stationery close to hand and, if necessary, slightly hide items or screens from view.
'Neat' desk organisers, prices on request, by Johan van Hengel, www.johanvanhengel.com

SSS **SIEDLE**

Watchful
on the outside.

Convenient
on the inside.

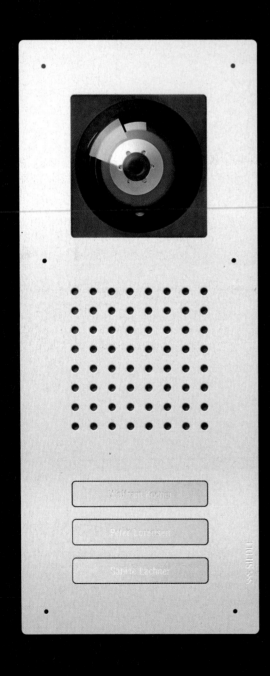

Siedle video
systems.

www.siedle.com

CLOCKWISE FROM TOP LEFT,
CANDLEHOLDER, PRICE ON
REQUEST, BY AFTEROOM. 'MODERN'
CUPBOARD, €4,181, BY PIERO
LISSONI, FOR PORRO. IN CUPBOARD,
'FACADE' VASE, €238, BY MARCO
GUAZZINI. 'STEEL PIPE' DRINKS
TROLLEY, €1,200, BY SHIRO
KURAMATA, FOR CAPPELLINI.
'LOLITA' CHAIR, £674, BY EMMANUEL
GALLINA, FOR PORADA. 'DIPPED
FRAME' RUG, €900 PER SQ M,
BY CC-TAPIS. 'FAN' TABLE, £1,295,
BY PIERO LISSONI, FOR DESALTO.
'COSMIC' PLATES, FROM £30,
BY DIESEL LIVING, FOR SELETTI

FOR STOCKISTS, SEE PAGE 224

DINING ROOM

Simplicity is the order of the day

PHOTOGRAPHY: LEONARDO SCOTTI INTERIORS: AMY HEFFERNAN

⬆ 'TRUE COLOUR' VASES
by Lex Pott

Dutch designer Lex Pott's fascination with materials and their natural forms is the basis of his intriguing vase collection. The eight cylinders feature copper, aluminium, brass and steel, paired with their oxidised counterparts. It's a collection that plays on contrasts, the shiny metals standing out against the tarnished pinks, greens and blues. *'True Colour' vases, €480 each, by Lex Pott, www.lexpott.nl*

⬆ 'ROCK' TABLE
by Jean-Marie Massaud

There is something majestic about Jean-Marie Massaud's 'Rock' table for MDF Italia. Its elegance stems from the contrast between the heavy base and the more delicate top, available in smoked glass and matt-lacquered MDF versions. The tabletop sits on a whopping piece of moulded ultra high-performance fibre-reinforced cement, in natural or grey finishes, with subtle colour variations resulting from the drying and maturation process.
'Rock' table, €2,029, by Jean-Marie Massaud, for MDF Italia, www.mdfitalia.it

⬅ 'TOUCHWOOD' CHAIR
by Lars Beller Fjetland

Italian manufacturer Discipline presented a varied offering, featuring playful yet beautiful designs. The standout piece was Norwegian designer Lars Beller Fjetland's 'Touchwood' stackable chair. In line with Discipline's mission to use only natural materials, 'Touchwood' comes in five delicious tones that emphasise the wood grain.
'Touchwood' chair, price on request, by Lars Beller Fjetland, for Discipline, www.discipline.eu

⬆ OIL PIPE, PITCHER, SUGAR CONTAINER AND POURER
by Aldo Bakker

Aldo Bakker scrutinised the Georg Jensen archives when designing a collection of his own for the brand, and the result is a modern tribute to the master Henning Koppel. The collection combines functional design with sculptural forms – we particularly admire the stark yet elegant oil pipe (above left).
€58–€295, by Aldo Bakker, for Georg Jensen Living, www.georgjensen.com

PHOTOGRAPHY: ANDREA GARUTI WRITER: ROSA BERTOLI

TERZANI
LA LUCE PENSATA

Volver, Breath of new *Light*

design Studio 14

terzani.com

CLOCKWISE FROM TOP LEFT, 'ISOLE' VASES, FROM €180, BY SAM BARON, FOR BOSA. 'ORPHEO' BED, PRICE ON REQUEST, BY FERRUCCIO LAVIANI, FOR LEMA. 'TRIBECA' DUVET COVER, €820; 'SHINE' SHEETS, €703 PER PAIR; 'LIPARI' PILLOWCASES, €199 PER PAIR, ALL BY QUAGLIOTTI. 'ISA' DRESSING TABLE, PRICE ON REQUEST, BY STUDIO IRVINE, FOR MARSOTTO EDIZIONI. BRUSHES, FROM £14.50, BOTH BY KOH-I-NOOR. 'PANAREA' CHAIR, €3,488, BY ALESSANDRO LA SPADA, FOR VISIONNAIRE. 'ARCHITECTURAL' FRUIT BOWL, PRICE ON REQUEST, BY TSUKASA GOTO & UP GROUP. 'KAZIMIR' BEDSIDE TABLE, PRICE ON REQUEST, BY LUCA TURRINI, FOR PRANDINA. *DESIGN NORDEST*, €21.50, BY MARCO ROMANELLI, PUBLISHED BY EDITRICE ABITARE SEGESTA, FROM L'ARCHIVOLTO. 'APPAREL' WARDROBE/ROOM DIVIDER, PROTOTYPE, BY VERA & KYTE. 'SPACE 3' RUG (SEEN REFLECTED IN MIRROR), €2,422 PER SQ M, BY JAN KATH

FOR STOCKISTS, SEE PAGE 224

BEDROOM

We've found space for both fantasy and function

PHOTOGRAPHY: LEONARDO SCOTTI INTERIORS: AMY HEFFERNAN

LAST CALL FOR

NWW DESIGN AWARD

THE AWARD FOR CREATIVE INTERIOR DESIGN
HEAD OF JURY 2014: ERWIN WURM
SUBMIT UNTIL 1.8.2014

nww-designaward.org

↑ 'PEG' MIRROR
by Nendo

We often marvel at Nendo's smart but simple design tricks. This year the studio expanded its 2013 'Peg' collection, in which structures and surfaces are placed in conversation with each other as chair and table legs extend discreetly upwards into seats and tabletops. True to form, the 'Peg' mirror features a small hole that reveals a detail of its construction.
'Peg' mirror, €1,700, by Nendo, for Cappellini, cappellini.it

↑ 'MOVE' ROCKING CHAIR
by Rossella Pugliatti

Rossella Pugliatti's reinvention of the rocking chair for Giorgetti is in equal parts ambitious and delightful. In her sinuous design, two interlocking wooden structures combine to form the seat and the rocking base. Made of 30 pieces of solid ash, the chair is available in three finishes, natural, anthracite grey and walnut painted.
'Move' rocking chair, from €13,072, by Rossella Pugliatti, for Giorgetti, www.giorgetti-spa.it

↑ 'JOY' BED
by Claesson Koivisto Rune

Swedish architecture and design practice Claesson Koivisto Rune's penchant for curves is put to the test in this bed for Arflex. 'Joy' balances rigorous lines with sensual curves. The wooden base appears to float, thanks to the almost invisible metal feet, while the backrest features a crescent of padding. Finishes include wenge and oak stains and black and white lacquered versions.
'Joy' bed, €4,815, by Claesson Koivisto Rune, for Arflex, www.arflex.it

→ 'DC1409' SCONCE
by Vincenzo De Cotiis

As well as presenting a host of new designs this year (including a coffee table for Wallpaper* Handmade – see next issue), architect Vincenzo De Cotiis has opened a second space in Milan, a large gallery that will showcase his Progetto Domestico limited-edition furniture collections. This sconce caught our eye, softly diffusing light with its different weights of mesh.
'DC1409' sconce, €15,000, by Vincenzo De Cotiis Progetto Domestico, progettodomestico.it

THE W* HOUSE

Drop in at The W* House, constantly refreshed
with the very latest design finds, for a room by
room tour of our dream digs. Wallpaper.com/whouse

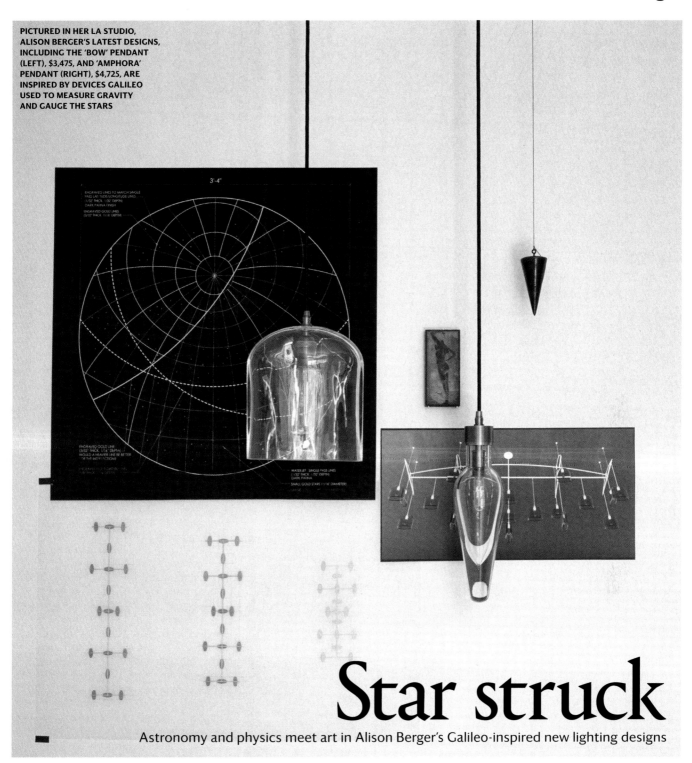

Star struck

Astronomy and physics meet art in Alison Berger's Galileo-inspired new lighting designs

In a world of uniform, mass-produced lighting, the works of Alison Berger stand apart. Over the last 20 years, the Texan-born, Los Angeles-based glass artist has created a unique collection of lighting and furniture at her eponymous studio. Berger relies on traditional glass-blowing techniques to shape unique, sculptural orbs that retain tool marks, fingerprints and bubbles as a stamp of authenticity. Crafted with precision, yet brimming over with character, her creations are both intriguing and familiar at the same time.

This year is set to be a bumper year for Berger; she's on course to release eight new lighting pieces in her biggest single release of new works to date. Her latest creations continue to articulate her artistic process while highlighting other sources of inspiration: science and history.

In all her pieces, Berger fuses up-to-date utilitarian function with an aspect of the past, a reverential gesture to the rites and rituals of a world gone by. Previous inspirations have included 4th-century wedding goblets, early industrial era troughs and Victorian cartographer tools. Her new lighting collection references the antique instruments and artifacts found in a catalogue from Florence's Museo Galileo,

including devices used by Galileo to calibrate the stars and to measure gravity.

'I really love how objects tell a story,' explains Berger. 'There's an underlying tone of anthropology and science to mine. I try to create atmospheric pieces that focus on the sculptural quality of light. The forms are historically based, but seem really new.'

Berger is the first to admit that her creations are in step with the nostalgia-oozing, heritage-tinged aesthetic in design that's so popular today. The point of distinction here is that no detail in Berger's work is superfluous. 'I remember going to flea markets when this style was becoming »

Design

and then began to pursue architecture at Columbia University. Her experience as an architect, first with Bausman-Gill Associates and then with Frank O Gehry & Associates, undoubtedly adds to her design rigour when it comes to lighting.

In her 'Bevel Sconce' light, featuring a skeletal bronze arm, the elliptical glass shade is blown so thickly and densely that the metal arm appears to succumb to the weight of the glass, like a tree branch bearing fruit. Another new piece, the 'Bow' pendant, which will also later be available as a five-arc chandelier, tricks the eye with its playful double profile; from the side it appears thin and angular, but when viewed from the front, it looks full and flat.

But Berger's designs are as much about the light as the form. 'The intention behind the pieces is for them to be left on throughout the day,' she says. 'They're atmospheric, meditative and sculptural, and are designed to look like they contain electric candlelight. A lot of the fixtures are fitted with a low, 25-watt bulb, but the truth is that the thickness of the crystal acts like a magnifying glass, making them appear brighter than they are. It's all about manipulating the glass to capture a different time of day in light. A chandelier, say, would be perfect with the kind of beautiful light you get at 5pm in the winter time, just as the sun is starting to fade.'

In Berger's hands, even a classic form such as the 'Amphora' pendant, which nods to Egyptian ointment jars, is transformed into something otherworldly. Matched with customised bronze fittings, its elongated form gently mimics the effect of watching rain coming through the light.

'I've been working with glass and light for so many years and I'm still shocked at what it does to me,' says Berger. 'From the cut of the glass to the object distortion and the mechanics, there are a lot of layers going on with every piece. When someone sees that, it feels successful.' ✱
www.alisonbergerglassworks.com

a look, and touching knobs and things, and then realising that they don't even work. For me, every part that has been created has a purpose,' she says, while describing the mechanics behind her 'Pulley' pendant, a hefty glass lantern counterbalanced by a slender strip of bronze wrapped in clear crystal. Attached to its counterweight by cables that run over bronze wheels, the lamp can be raised or lowered as required.

'It's a very precise piece that was inspired by the devices people were using to measure gravity,' says Berger. 'It's all about balance and calibration. There's a whole mathematical equation involved to balance the weight of the pulley with the pendant.'

One aspect of Berger's work that truly stands out is her ability to bend glass to her will and leave evidence of that process. 'All the pieces I do really capture the quality of handmade glasswork,' she explains. 'I make sure to keep all the markings and bubbles, because I don't want the glass to look plastic.'

Working without the use of moulds or form constraints, Berger coaxes her shapes out of glass, blowing each piece by hand. No two pieces are ever alike. It's a skill that is second nature to the artist, who began blowing glass as a teenager in her home town of Dallas. She went on to study sculpture at the Rhode Island School of Design, before moving to New York to apprentice with the renowned glass artist Dale Chihuly,

meTime_spa

FITTING FOR THE SENSES

meTime_spa: Based on an architecturally orientated interior design style, the innovative range of fittings for the shower and bath tub reflect the highest level of creativity and individuality. The glass panel comes in various sizes and, besides chrome-plated control elements to adjust the flow and temperature of the water, it also offers aluminium shelving. **www.keuco.de**

THE VITRAHAUS EXHIBITION, CURATED BY ILSE CRAWFORD, TAKES THE FORM OF AN APARTMENT LIVED IN BY A FICTIONAL CREATIVE COUPLE, ASTRID AND HARRI. THERE'S A CORK MOODBOARD, WHILE 'TRAPÈZE' TABLES, BY JEAN PROUVÉ, ALLOW THE COUPLE TO WORK SIDE BY SIDE, ON CHARLES AND RAY EAMES' 'SOFT PAD' CHAIRS, BOTH FOR VITRA. ALSO PICTURED IS VITRA'S 'NELSON BENCH', BY GEORGE NELSON. FROM THE CEILING HANG A BAMBOO SCULPTURE BY MIE MATSUBARA AND A POLYSTYRENE CHAIN, BY SUZANNE STANKUS

TIMELINE ILLUSTRATOR: THE LUXURY OF PROTEST

VITRA

VITRA DEUTSCHLAND FOUNDED IN WEIL AM RHEIN
By Willi and Erika Fehlbaum • 1950

STARTS PRODUCTION OF THE HERMAN MILLER COLLECTION
Including products from Charles and Ray Eames, Isamu Noguchi and George Nelson

THE PANTON CHAIR LAUNCHED • 1967
The first cantilevered chair made out of plastic, by Verner Panton

A FIRE DESTROYS A LARGE PART OF THE PRODUCTION FACILITIES IN WEIL AM RHEIN • 1981

FRANK GEHRY MEETS ROLF FEHLBAUM AND A PLURALIST CONCEPT FOR THE ARCHITECTURAL DEVELOPMENT OF THE VITRA CAMPUS IS INTRODUCED • 1984

FRANK GEHRY FINISHES VITRA DESIGN MUSEUM AS PART OF THE CAMPUS • 1989

ZAHA HADID'S FIRE STATION COMPLETE, AS WELL AS TADAO ANDO'S CONFERENCE PAVILION, ALSO ON THE CAMPUS • 1993

LAUNCH OF HOME COLLECTION • 2004
Classic products from Charles and Ray Eames, George Nelson, Verner Panton and Jean Prouvé, as well as new pieces from Jasper Morrison, Maarten van Severen, Ronan and Erwan Bouroullec, Hella Jongerius and Edward Barber and Jay Osgerby

VITRAHAUS OPENS • 2010
Part of the Vitra campus, flagship store and home of the Vitra Home Collection Designed by Herzog & de Meuron

VITRA ACQUIRES ARTEK • 2013

JOINT CONCEPT SHOP OPENS IN BERLIN • 2014

ARTEK

BENT L-LEG STOOL PATENTED
BY ALVAR AALTO • 1933
Solid wood leg, bent 90 degrees

ARTEK FOUNDED • 1935
By Alvar and Aino Aalto, Nils-Gustav Hahl and Maire Gullichsen

RESTAURANT SAVOY HELSINKI • 1937
With interior design by Aino Aalto and customised furniture by Artek

LAUNCH OF Y-LEG • 1946
Used in chairs and tables, with two 90 degree bends. Originally made from an L-Leg sawn in two

LAUNCH OF X-LEG • 1954
Fan-shaped leg made from sawing an L-Leg into five parts. Now made from a laminated bend, dowelled into seats or tabletops • 1992

SWEDISH INVESTMENT COMPANY PROVENTUS ACQUIRES ARTEK • 2004

TOM DIXON CREATIVE DIRECTOR • 2005

MIRKKU KULLBERG APPOINTED MANAGING DIRECTOR • 2007

ARTEK PAVILION AT SALONE DEL MOBILE IN MILAN DESIGNED BY SHIGERU BAN
Later moved to Helsinki, between the Museum of Finnish Architecture and the Design Museum, and then reconstructed at Design Miami

ARTEK IS ACQUIRED BY VITRA BUT CONTINUES TO BE MARKETED AS A SEPARATE ENTITY • 2013

lvar Aalto was never a Finnish designer,' says Mirkku Kullberg, the straight-talking CEO of Artek, the furniture company founded by the late modernist master. 'He was a universal designer, and we need to try to take these legacy companies out of their national context and bring them to an international audience and platform.' Kullberg followed her own advice when, early in 2013, she picked up the phone and rang the Swiss design giant Vitra.

On the other end of the connection was Nora Fehlbaum, a member of Vitra's board of directors, who left a job in consulting to join the family business in 2010. (Her uncle is Rolf Fehlbaum, chairman emeritus, active member of the board of directors and Vitra's long-time patron saint, who managed the company for decades until stepping back from daily business operations in 2005.)

Kullberg soon discovered that the admiration was mutual and, in early September last year, Vitra acquired Artek from Proventus, a Swedish private equity firm that had held the Finnish company in its portfolio for some 20 years.

And so, without much fanfare, a new chapter began for both companies: Vitra would provide Artek with an international platform that would enable it to grow and develop and to take advantage of economies of scale when it came to manufacturing, distribution and logistics. Artek, in turn, would add icons of the Scandinavian modernist movement to Vitra's already impressive design hall of fame, which runs from Charles and Ray Eames and Jean Prouvé through to Jasper Morrison and the Bouroullec brothers.

Some eight months into this new partnership, both women are seated in a meeting room on the Vitra Campus in the small German town of Weil am Rhein, the landscape dotted with buildings and works by Frank Gehry, Tadao Ando, Zaha Hadid, SANAA, and many more.

Kullberg has spent nearly a decade with Artek, moving the brand into the 21st century, and inviting contemporary »

IN THE FICTIONAL COUPLE'S
APARTMENT ARE 'STOOL',
BY CHARLES AND RAY EAMES;
'PLACE' SOFA AND 'CORK FAMILY'
STOOLS, BY JASPER MORRISON;
AND 'AKARI' LIGHTING BY ISAMU
NOGUCHI, ALL FOR VITRA, AS
WELL AS 'ARMCHAIR 400',
BY ALVAR AALTO, FOR ARTEK

LEFT, ILSE CRAWFORD AT
STUDIOILSE IN LONDON. HER
TEAM'S GOAL WAS TO VISUALISE
THE UNION OF THE SWISS
AND FINNISH BRANDS

PHOTOGRAPHY: WILLIAM SELDEN

designers like Hella Jongerius and Konstantin Grcic to, respectively, reinterpret classic designs and create new ones. (Grcic's 'Rival' task chair was launched at Salone this year.) In the process, Kullberg has taken Artek from a slightly forgotten Finnish legacy brand to an international design company. The Vitra sale was perhaps an obvious next step.

'It was time for Artek to make a move and we thought about who could help take us forward in an interesting way,' says Kullberg. 'It had to be someone who understood the products and what it meant to work with design classics, and Vitra seemed quite obvious in that sense.'

The Vitra deal wasn't without its detractors, though. Some homegrown sceptics practically accused Kullberg of selling off a piece of Finnish national heritage. 'Of course it's our obligation to look after this national treasure,' says Kullberg. 'But at the same time, it's also our obligation to keep on supporting the really rather radical ideals that Artek was

founded around: bringing new things to new people – and I think this is where Vitra will really push us forward.'

Founded in Finland in 1935, Artek – a literal fusion of the words art and technology – was the brainchild of architect Alvar Aalto and his wife Aino, art historian Nils-Gustav Hahl and art promoter Maire Gullichsen. It was born of an ambition to promote a modern approach to living through a furniture and lighting collection, as well as through exhibitions and educational programmes. Today, the collection extends far beyond Aalto's own designs and includes pieces by Finnish greats including Ilmari Tapiovaara and Yrjö Kukkapuro, as well as works by Grcic, Jongerius and Shigeru Ban.

'This is really about allowing Artek to continue this progression,' says Fehlbaum. 'We don't want it to be that we brought a status quo in 2013, integrated and that was that. Vitra and Artek undeniably have values in common, which is what makes this work.

Both companies have humble beginnings among family and friends, and we have both showed a lifelong commitment to education, consistently engaging in a dialogue about what good design means. But while we have ideas in common, we are very careful and adamant about having separate collections: Artek will remain a separate institution and have its own brand identity.' Proof of this commitment to independence arguably came at this year's Salone del Mobile, when Artek and Vitra showed their work from separate stands.

But that isn't to say that Kullberg and Fehlbaum want to downplay the compatibility of the two collections: to formally introduce the partnership to the public, Kullberg and Fehlbaum invited Ilse Crawford's team at Studioilse to curate and design an exhibition that would visualise the marriage of the two companies.

It seems fitting then that Crawford temporarily transformed the loft on the top

floor of the Herzog & de Meuron-designed VitraHaus into the flat of a fictitious couple: Harri, a Finnish musician, and Astrid, a German set designer. The results are seamless and Vitra's diverse collection, from Jasper Morrison's 'Cork' stools to Frank Gehry's 'Wiggle' side chair, plays well with the Finnish additions. Perhaps most poetic is the dialogue between each brand's hero figure – throughout the space Eames and Aalto sit in conversation, and it feels entirely organic, obvious, maybe even meant to be.

'The two companies are really well-matched in terms of their integrity,' says Crawford. 'I think Vitra has more muscle

'It's like the perfect marriage: they both want to be more like the other one'

than Artek because of its sheer size, but you could argue that Artek has more soul because it's smaller and closer to the root, and it has a very domestic application. It's the perfect marriage really: they both want to be more like the other one is, but they have enough in common to make them a compatible couple.'

This April, the two companies opened their first joint-venture, a concept shop in Berlin, and their partnership will, of course, be increasingly visible, with all Vitra showrooms carrying the Artek collection. In some instances, as in Japan and Finland, where Artek has a strong hold, Artek outlets will also offer Vitra's home collection.

The question is briefly floated, whether this might be the start of an acquisition strategy for Vitra. The notion is quickly quelled by Fehlbaum, however, who notes that the company has never acquired before, and wouldn't have, had it not been Artek who called: 'Right down to the font of our

logos to the five letters of our names, we have so much in common. This was possible because it was really a loving relationship, and those aren't easy to replicate – there needs to be that spark for something like this to work,' says Fehlbaum.

For now, both Kullberg and Fehlbaum agree, it's really about getting back to business. After a year of big changes, the year ahead will be spent on product development, fine-tuning retail strategies, and putting the focus back on selling the product.

'We kind of have this mantra at Artek, for people coming into the business,' says Kullberg. 'You have two minutes to sell yourself to the company, and then you have the rest of your life to sell the product,' she explains, revealing an inter-company mantra that seems to have become a self-fulfilling prophecy. 'Sell the company, sell the thinking, and then it all starts happening.' ✱
Vitra Artek, Bikini House, Budapester Strasse 38-50, Berlin, www.artek.fi, www.vitra.com

NIKE'S MAGISTA BOOT USES
FLYKNIT TECHNOLOGY FOR
AN ULTRA-LIGHT 'SOCK' FIT

OPPOSITE, MARTIN LOTTI,
NIKE'S FOOTBALL GLOBAL
CREATIVE DIRECTOR

Kick off

After four years of research and 180 prototypes,
Nike releases a football boot that ticks all the right boxes

PHOTOGRAPHY: NICHOLAS ALAN COPE   WRITER: SIMON MILLS

A FEW OF THE 180 PROTOTYPES
FOR THE MAGISTA BOOT, SHOWING
ITS SOCK-LIKE COLLAR, AND,
BOTTOM RIGHT, ONE OF THE
FINISHED FORMS. AVAILABLE FROM
$75 TO $325, WWW.NIKE.COM

Like the FIFA World Cup itself, Nike's soccer boot concepts tend to operate within a four-year cycle. Creative director Martin Lotti and his staff at Nike started work on 2014's revolutionary new Magista boot back in 2010, straight after the last ball had been kicked at the Soccer City-stadium final in Johannesburg. 'We began with a blank sheet of paper,' says Lotti. 'We asked ourselves, if we were designing a football boot completely from scratch, without any knowledge of what had gone before, how would it look?'

This policy of year-zero radicalism prevails everywhere at Nike headquarters. Lotti is into collaborative cross-pollination and wall-length moodboards, seeking influence from beyond the conventional sporting arena. 'We will look at anything and everything except the category that we will be working on. If we're going to design shoes, we're going to look at anything but shoes. That way you're more likely to end up setting trends rather than chasing them.'

So, before a single sketch was made, a rendering submitted or a CAD drawing uploaded for the Magista project, Lotti arranged a trip to Iceland to look at nature – geysers, icebergs, glaciers and molten magma – and then onto Paris to immerse his creative team in architecture. 'We look at culture, geography, buildings and people and translate it all into product.'

This is a tactically astute game plan that has worked for Nike before. Back in 2002, during a visit to Kyoto, Lotti conceived Nike's first ever yoga shoe after becoming entranced by the 'fine lines, beauty, simplicity and grace' of the Zen gardens and watching, mesmerised, as young people dressed in kimonos walked into temples.

In 1988, Tinker Hatfield, Nike's legendary vice president for design and special projects (originally hired by the sportswear behemoth as its 'corporate architect' to work on its shops and offices), had been similarly fired up by the sight of the externalised heating ducts, exposed metal bracings and denuded lift shafts on Richard Rogers and Renzo Piano's Centre Pompidou in Paris. Back at his Oregon atelier, Hatfield dug out a panel from the Nike Air Max 1's sole wall to reveal the bubbled cushioning inside. Lotti, in turn, cites Frank Gehry's Guggenheim Museum in Bilbao as an influence on the audacious Magista design. 'It's a stark example of a piece of architecture that's strong and substantial but also has grace and soft fluidity.'

Of course, Nike also consulted its stellar roster of brand ambassadors and sponsored footballers during the 180-prototype research and development process. Initially, the question was as wide open as the last ten minutes of a cup final: 'What do you want from a football boot?'

Quickly, a podiatric mantra of 'fit, touch and traction' emerged. The likes of Brazil's Neymar and Spain's Iniesta, club colleagues at FC Barcelona, talked of a desire to play barefoot. (Or at least to mimic that liberated sensation through their footwear.) The dazzling pace and intensity of the modern game was discussed: a need for a shoe that could slow down a game enough for the ball to be controlled and then speed it up again. 'This is all done in one moment,' says Lotti. 'There's no time to settle, take a touch and then pass or shoot. It's not a conscious thing or reasoned thought process. It happens instinctively. We knew we had to make a boot that was similarly fluid, a true extension of the foot. The player and the shoe becoming one.' Then, a pro footballer – Lotti claims he doesn't remember exactly who – delivered the definitive craving. 'What I really want,' said the striker, 'is a sock with cleats.'

'We now had a clear vision of where we wanted to go,' says Lotti, grinning broadly.

'What I really want,' said the striker, 'is a sock with cleats'

Weapons-grade hosiery – a sock-a-boot, if you will – armoured and weatherproofed but super-light and engineered for goals was the way forward. Nike looked at the form of a glove, the way that it supports a hand beyond the wrist, and adapted the concept for the foot. Nike turned to its Flyknit material, born of a micro-level process that employs computer-controlled 'knitting' technology to form a shoe upper with woven strands of polyester. 'By using different yarns of differing strengths, stretch and flexibility, Flyknit allows us to engineer each boot differently,' says Lotti. The complete shoe upper emerges from the multiple-spooled weaving machine and there's none of the last-making, templating and cutting out you associate with conventional cobbling.

Certainly, Nike and Wallpaper* are in the right place to discuss the technicalities of the beautiful game. Our interview with Lotti takes place in a VVIP box high up in the bleachers at Barcelona's Camp Nou stadium. The magnificent ground is deserted right now, but the palpably theatrical atmosphere it generates helped convince Nike to make a boot that would deliver not just control and goals but would also engender an emotional connection and generate a visceral reaction to its performance.

Months ago, key Barcelona players were involved in highly covert testing trials of the Magista/Playmaker boot (actually part of Nike's four-strong, discipline-adjusted, six-yard box assault of footwear that also includes Hypervenom/Attack, Mercurial/Speed and Tiempo/Touch).

Testing was done over a three-year period. 'We had 140 testers,' recalls Lotti. 'More than 3,000 hours on the pitch. And some players refused to give back the shoes when the test was over.' He was at the training ground when a Barcelona pro scored a goal for the very first time wearing the finished Magista 'sock-with-cleats' boot. 'A clean low strike in from outside the penalty area, right into the bottom corner,' beams Lotti. 'It was quite a moment.' *

Hiéronyme Lacroix and Simon Chessex set up their office in Geneva in 2005, having begun their careers with stints in various architecture firms in Switzerland and New York, including a spell at Herzog & de Meuron for Chessex and time with Rogers Marvel architects for Lacroix. Their own work has seen them building at a variety of scales, always taking the very pragmatic (and very Swiss) view that each job is a blank slate for just the right approach. Major projects such as new student lodgings in Geneva – an elegant slab apartment block – contrast strongly with the refurbishment and extension of a chalet in Gryon, where their compact new wooden element forms a tailored appendage to the more traditional original structure.

A new house takes their interest in vernacular architecture one step further. Les Jeurs is the archetypal Alpine village, a small community nestling in the thickly forested mountains above route D1506, the road that runs between the French resort of Chamonix and the Swiss town of Martigny. For centuries, such hamlets have been built along similar lines, with traditional wooden houses erected on cleared meadows made from the flattest part of the wooded hillsides. This is a predominantly agricultural region, and storage for animals, equipment and foodstuffs has resulted in the creation of a hybrid structure – houses elevated above hay barns, with a clear separation between the two structures.

The new house sits on a slight promontory at the end of a private drive. Half the plot is steep hillside, and the new house is perched right at the edge of the slope. The basement level, cast in solid concrete, is a direct reference to those ancient hay barns. 'In these, the wood construction was lifted above ground and separated by a round stone that prevented mice from getting in and eating the grain,' the architects explain. 'In our project, the »

concrete plinth and cantilevers are a kind of reinterpretation of this expression of a "flying wooden house", detached from the ground.' The effect is made all the more dramatic by the way the house seems to step, just slightly, over the edge of the ridge.

The house itself is formed by two interlocking structures, one set at a 45 degree angle to the other, creating what the architects describe as an 'Alpine shape'. The form is simultaneously a maquette of a mountain landscape and a self-contained village, the pattern of roofs and façades making a pleasing punctuation point on the terrain. 'The project questions the shape and the scale of the traditional little mountain constructions,' say the architects, producing a series of animations to illustrate how the programme is neatly spliced in two, a device

that allows for unpredictable viewing angles both into and out of the house.

The plan breaks up the mass, so the three-bedroom house doesn't appear overbearing. Depending on where you're standing in the valley – down below or high above – it appears much smaller than it really is, even reading as two separate volumes from some angles, all the while retaining the archetypal 'house' shape of a pitched roof above a rectangular volume. It's severe, stark even, with a green tint to the vertical wooden cladding that keeps the structure within the region's distinctive Alpine palette.

Inside, it's another story. Large picture windows, especially in the jutting cantilevered section, bring the spectacular surroundings to life. Windows also mediate the relationship between the house's

interlinked structures, setting up a dialogue between each element. The walls, ceilings and floors are all made from one material – fir. 'It's a clear strategy not to make any difference between floors, walls and ceilings,' the architects explain, 'so that the space is really highlighted by natural light.' That light floods in through the frameless windows, while components like the staircase and integral benches give the house a feeling of solidity, as if the entire interior has been carved from a solid block of wood.

The result is a house that doesn't startle with its modernity, but works in harmony with its surroundings. It's not just a frame for the landscape outside, but a vessel for the life within, its fractured plan serving as a constant reminder of place. ★
www.lacroixchessex.ch

SHIFT no. 6
FROM SOLITUDE TO MULTITUDE

Society is actually becoming more secluded since, to a large extent, work is the only place where we integrate and cooperate with other people. Broadly speaking, the workplace is changing from a place of tasks to a place of projects. Kinnarps Trend Report – 8 shifts affecting the workplace of tomorrow. See the full report at **www.kinnarps.com/trend**

Making life better at work

THE WINNER OF
THE SOFITEL MYBED
UNIVERSE COMPETITION,
'SLEEP SPACE', BY
FRENCH DESIGNER
CLÉMENTINE PAUTROT

SLEEPING BEAUTY

Insomniacs beware. It might be all too easy to slumber for a hundred
years on the winning design of the Sofitel MyBed Universe competition

PHOTOGRAPHY: CHRISTIAN HAGEMANN SET BUILD: STUDIO NITZAN COHEN

Driven by a fantasy of sleeping outdoors, surrounded by water, Clémentine Pautrot's winning creation for the Sofitel MyBed Universe competition is simple but poetic. The competition, launched earlier this year by Wallpaper* and the Sofitel hotel brand, urged designers to turn their wildest nocturnal fancies into reality. With Sofitel's MyBed products at the core of all creations, entrants were asked to design the ultimate sleeping environment.

The designers faced a number of challenges when conceiving such a space. 'It's about finding the right balance between functionality, design and comfort,' says competition judge Rick Harvey Lam, Accor* Group's senior vice-president of global marketing for luxury and upscale brands. 'The bed takes centre stage and the rest of the space must be structured around it.' The remaining judges, interior designer Nicolas

Adnet, of Studio MHNA, interior architect Hervé Van der Straeten, Wallpaper* creative director Sarah Douglas and Grégoire Champetier, Accor chief of marketing, were also looking for originality, functionality and comfort. An environment that surprises, declutters and looks beautiful.

With hotels in America, Asia and Europe, and its portfolio rapidly expanding, Sofitel puts culture and design to the fore across its various brands. The brand has a tradition of collaborating with well-known designers and architects; Sofitels have been designed with the likes of Studio Putman, Jean Nouvel, Christian Lacroix and Karl Lagerfeld.

With its MyBed concept, Sofitel dovetails design and luxury, offering guests a bespoke mattress, base and featherbed combination, developed by luxury bedding specialists Epeda and Dumas with bed linens by Yves Delorme. Sofitel chose Wallpaper*, a global authority on

design, travel and fine bed linen, as the perfect partner and platform for this project.

Exploring the notion of sleep as a magical experience, Pautrot's installation captures that mysterious phase between falling asleep and dreaming. 'The ladder represents the upward journey into the delirious dream state,' she explains. The ladder was handmade by artisan metalworkers in solid brass tubing. Wallpaper* and creative directors Studio Nitzan Cohen then brought the bedscape to life as the centrepiece for a cocktail event at Sofitel Munich Bayerpost in April.

Pautrot studied interior design at École Supérieure des Arts et Techniques in Paris, and currently works for Risch Erlingsen Design, a small agency specialising in merchandising for luxury brands. 'I see interior design as a way to improve people's lives,' she says. Even when they are asleep. *www.sofitel.com, www.soboutique.com*

THIS PAGE, THE STONE
PATHWAY THAT LEADS
TO THE SLEEPING AREA
IN PAUTROT'S DESIGN

OPPOSITE, THE
DESIGNER WITH HER
'DREAM LADDER'

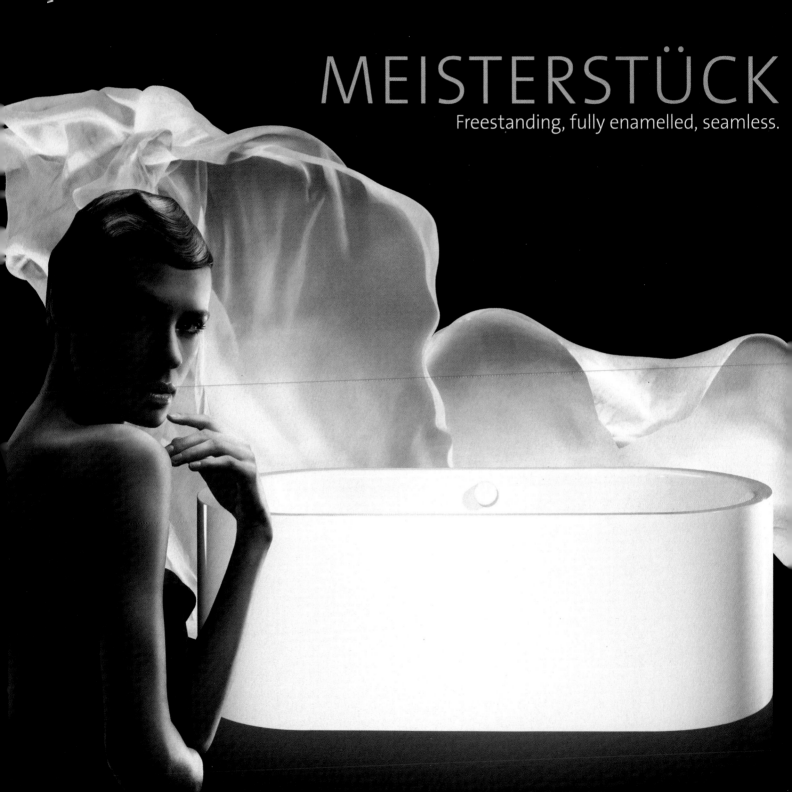

K&B 2014

Kitchen & Bathroom Digest

Our annual nod to the smart and the superior brings you everything from an outdoor shower pavilion to a transparent tap and a Corten tub; plus crucial kitchens, an invisible dishwasher, a countertop herb garden and a wonder hob

sophisticated since 1908

unique® by eggersmann

eggersmann.com

Sophisticated simplicity

+SEGMENTO

The simplest appearance often belies the most complex thinking. +**SEGMENTO**'s exquisite and simple design hides decades of thought and experience. Thin worktops, handle-less surfaces and a purity of lines combine to refine the visual experience.

Poggenpohl Möbelwerke GmbH
Poggenpohlstraße 1
D-32051 Herford
Fon +49 (0) 5221 / 381 -0
info@poggenpohl.com
www.poggenpohl.com

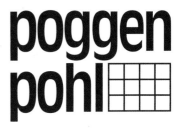

Kaohsiung City | Taiwan

www.leicht.com

Function. Elegance. Harmony.

LEICHT®

TOILETTEPAPER*

*The best new ablution solutions for your bathroom

'WAZEBO' OUTDOOR SHOWER PAVILION, PRICE ON REQUEST, BY LUDOVICA & ROBERTO PALOMBA, FOR ZUCCHETTI.KOS. 'SCALETTA' RADIATOR, PRICE ON REQUEST, BY ELISA GIOVANNONI, FOR TUBES RADIATORI. 'PLISSNEW' TOWELS, £165 PER PAIR, BY SOCIETY. STOOL, €6,300, BY SHIGEO MASHIRO, FOR SFERA. SOAP, £1; SOAP DISH, £4; BATH SALTS, £6, IN BOTTLE, £3.50; LIQUID SOAPS, £5 EACH, ALL BY MUJI. 'TIERRAS' FLOORING, €400 PER SQ M, BY PATRICIA URQUIOLA, FOR MUTINA

FOR STOCKISTS, SEE PAGE 054

Dornbracht
Horizontal Shower ATT

dornbracht.com/horizontal-shower   mail@dornbrachtgroup.de
Product Design   Sieger Design

Culturing Life

⬇ 'CYPRUM' TAP
by Dornbracht

The gold tap has had a long if checkered history since its 1970s heyday, while copper has more recent design credentials, making a big splash at design fairs in 2011 (W*143) and hardly waning in popularity since. Dornbracht's rose gold 'Cyprum' tap is the best of both worlds: a reflective finish made from 18-carat gold and genuine copper.
'Cyprum' tap, price on request, by Dornbracht, www.dornbracht.com

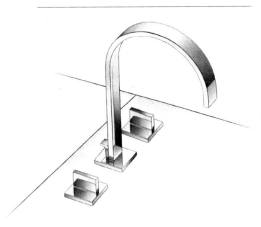

⬇ 'CONTROSTAMPO' BATHTUB
by Vittorio Venezia

Last year, Vittorio Venezia's 'Controstampo' moulded bathroom collection won first prize in the Falper-sponsored Cristalplant Design Contest. Now the Sicilian designer's bath and basin have made it into the catalogue of the Bologna-based bathroom specialist. The rusted Corten finish is obtained by oxidising metallic paint, which is then sealed with a transparent coating.
'Controstampo' bathtub, €8,616, by Vittorio Venezia, for Falper, www.falper.it

⬆ 'IL BAGNO' COLLECTION
by Antonio Lupi

Tuscan brand Antonio Lupi's new bathroom collection, 'Il Bagno' designed by Roberto Lazzeroni, transforms a typically clinical space into a homely sanctuary. Functional bathroom fittings have become furnishings with romantic lines, warm wood finishing, coloured lacquered surfaces and midcentury details. Lazzeroni has drawn on the brand's 50-year history to integrate classic, elegant aesthetics into the new collection, at times updating vintage designs, such as 1950s mirrors, with contemporary materials. The whole collection brings the look and feel of the living room to the bathroom and, as a result, encourages long, lingering ablutions.
'Il Bagno' collection, from €4,800 for the composition pictured, by Roberto Lazzeroni, for Antonio Lupi, www.antoniolupi.it

PHOTOGRAPHY: DANIELE DE CAROLIS ILLUSTRATOR: MAGDA ANTONIUK WRITERS: SUJATA BURMAN, EMMA MOORE

Bathroom News

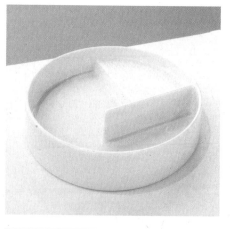

⬆ SINKSIDE TRAY
by Konstantin Grcic

Designers Konstantin Grcic and Toan Nguyen have been testing the boundaries of Laufen's durable and malleable new ceramic-based material SaphirKeramik. Nguyen moulded it into paper thin curves for his sink unit, while Grcic's series of washbasins and sinkside trays (pictured) demonstrate how it adapts to graphic forms and decoration. *Sinkside tray, prototype, to be launched in 2015, by Konstantin Grcic, for Laufen, www.laufen.com*

⬇ 'AXOR STARCK V' TAP
by Philippe Starck

It was the patriarch of the Hansgrohe family tap business, Klaus Grohe, who suggested that long-time collaborator Philippe Starck explore a see-through device for them. It was Grohe too, who realised that such a tap could showcase the strangely hypnotic vortex of water it funnels. The resultant design has practical benefits as well as aesthetic – the entire unit can be removed for cleaning. *'Axor Starck V' tap, price on request, by Philippe Starck, for Hans Grohe, www.hansgrohe.com*

⬆ SAUNA AND STEAM BATH
by Matteo Thun and Antonio Rodriguez

Expert in the art of relaxation, German sauna, pool and spa accessory manufacturer Klafs is soothing body and mind with a pared back new sauna and steam room duo. Drawn up by Matteo Thun and Antonio Rodriguez, the freestanding, cubic cabins filter in plenty of natural light while offering seclusion from the outside world. The sauna (pictured) is composed of glass fronted by slatted hemlock, oak or walnut, while the all-white steam room, made of glass and quartz agglomerate, achieves a similar effect with opalescent strips across its front. To ensure minds are kept untroubled, all signs of technology are well concealed. *Sauna and steam bath, from €20,000 each, by Matteo Thun an Antonio Rodriguez, for Klafs, www.klafs.com*

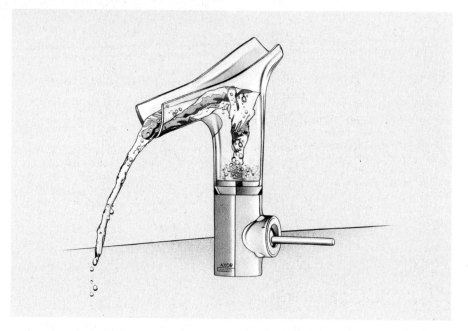

PHOTOGRAPHY: DANIELE DE CAROLIS ILLUSTRATOR: MAGDA ANTONIUK

**THE BATHROOM.
BY PHILIPPE STARCK.**

Design by Philippe Starck

25
YEARS
COOPERATION
STARCK
+DURAVIT

More nuances. More elegance. More versatility: The Starck bathroom series with the coordinating furniture programme. Just one example from the comprehensive Duravit range – sanitary ceramics, bathroom furniture, accessories, bathtubs, wellness products and saunas. Free brochure available from Duravit AG, export@duravit.de, **www.duravit.com**

Face and eye essence, £60 for 50ml, by **Dr Jackson's**, from **Net-a-Porter**. Black Amber, £125 for 50ml, by **Agonist Parfums**, from **The Conran Shop**. Konjac sponge, €7, by **Nomess**. Infused facial water, £35 for 150ml, by **Diptyque**. 'Solid' mirror, price on request, by **Diego Vencato and Marco Merendi**, for **Agape**. 'Surf' washbasin and countertop, price on request, by **Andrea Bassanello**, for **Modulnova**. 'Venezia' tap, £1,780, by **Matteo Thun and Antonio Rodriguez**, for **Fantini**. Camphor stone soap, £16, by **Pelle**, from **The Conran Shop**. Acrylic container with gold handle, £69, by **Decor Walther**.

Black cotton buds, €3, by **Nomess**. 'Finferli' hooks, €36 each, by **Note Design Studio**, for **Ex.t**. 'Shade' folding screen, from £3,355, by **Marco Taietta**, for **Makro**. Bamboo wash belt, £23, from **Balineum**. Body lotion; conditioner, £10 each for 150ml, by **Ila**. 'DR' bathtub, price on request, by **Studio MK27**, for **Agape**. Free-standing bath mixer, £3,670, by **Aarhus Arkitekterne**, for **Vola**. 'TT' radiator, price on request, by **Matteo Thun and Antonio Rodriguez**, for **Antrax IT**. 'Picture Gallery Red' estate emulsion, £36 per 2.5 litres, by **Farrow & Ball**. 'Blend' floor tiles, price on request, by **Marazzi**

Dark materials

Bathrooms are showing their masculine side

PHOTOGRAPHY: LUKE KIRWAN INTERIORS: MARIA SOBRINO

'Lago' wall lights in bronze, from £120 each, by **Astro Lighting**. 'Crosscut' mirrors, £165 each, by **Faudet-Harrison**, for **SCP**. Double washbasin with soft-close drawers and single-lever mixers, £8,170, by **Armani/Roca**. Anti-aging cream, £85, by **Algenist**, from **Space NK**. Serums, from a selection, by **Codage**, from **Selfridges**. Sponges, £26 for six, from **Liberty**. Powder brush and make-up, from a selection, by **MAC Cosmetics**. Accessory set (toothbrush holder, soap dispenser, soap dish, tissue box holder), £960, by **Armani/Roca**. 'Nebula' scent diffuser, price on request, by **Studio WM**. 'Puck' table with polished copper top, £450, by **Simen Aarseth**, for **Benchmark**. Towel rail, £248, by **Armani/Roca**. Kontex face towel, £36, by **Morihata**, from **Liberty**. 'Mole's Breath' estate emulsion, £36 per 2.5 litres, by **Farrow & Ball**. 'Authentic Wood' floor in tan, £50 per sq m, by **Harvey Maria**

'Closer' showerhead, price on request, by **Diego Grandi**, for **Zucchetti**. 'Xenon' concealed shower trim set in matt black chrome, £492, by **Samuel Heath**. 'Scona' shower tray, £661, by **Kaldewei**. 'I Frammenti' tiles in silver, €452 per sq m, by **Claudio Silvestrin**, for **Brix**. Coco Mademoiselle scented foam bath, £75 for 400ml, by **Chanel**. Natural sea sponge, €11, by **Compagnie de Provence**, from **Aria**. Simulated ivory bath brush, £125, by **Geo F Trumper**. Ecopelle hamper, £145, by **Koh-I-Noor**. Toilet paper holder, ¥30,000 ($295), by **Kanaya**, for **Mikiya Kobayashi**. Toilet paper, €7 for six rolls, by **Renova**. M-Line wall-hung WC, £300, by **NOA**, for **VitrA**. Flush plate, £95, by **Toto**, from **CP Hart**. 'Bin 3' in black, €220, by **Decor Walther**. 'System Fit' washbasin unit in grey oak, from £831, by **Nexus**, for **VitrA**. Regenerating plant oil, £43 for 125ml, by **Christophe Robin**. Toothpaste, £3, by **Couto**. Black bristle toothbrush, £5, by **Nomess**. Dry oil spray; body lotion, from £30, both by **Hotel Costes**, from **Net-a-Porter**. 'Venna 60' wall light, €418, by **Decor Walther**. Square copper washbasin, part of the Water Jewels collection, from £564, by **VitrA**. 'Tara' basin mixer in matt black, £849, by **Dornbracht**, from **CP Hart**. 'Bowl' mirror in gloss rose, €805, by **Arik Levy**, for **Inbani**. 'Tetro' radiator, £1,044, by **Bisque**. 'Paulistano' chair, £1,375, by **Paulo Mendes da Rocha**, for **Objekto**, from **Twentytwentyone**. Revive bath towel, £13, from **Christy**. 'Mole's Breath' estate emulsion, £36 per 2.5 litres, by **Farrow & Ball**. 'Blend' floor tiles, price on request, by **Marazzi**. Wood stain in teak, from £25 for 750ml, by **Earthborn Paints**

Wash unit (featuring mirror, tray, tap, washbasin and drawers), part of the Dressage collection, price on request, by **Studio Nespoli e Novara**, for **Graff**. Ebony military hairbrush, £60, by **Geo F Trumper**. Amber massage oil, £25, by **Côté Bastide**, from **The Conran Shop**. 'Cibele' free-standing bath, €7,100; 'Narciso' tray with mirror (over bath), €300, both by **Ceramica Cielo**. Hair conditioners, €36 each, by **BIO A+OE**. 'Picture Gallery Red' estate emulsion, £36 per 2.5 litres, by **Farrow & Ball**. 'Authentic Wood' floor in tan, £50 per sq m, by **Harvey Maria**

For stockists, see page 054

IN-TANK. THE FIRST WC TO HAVE
THE CISTERN INCORPORATED WITHIN IT.

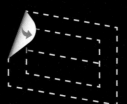

Roca presents the WC of the future.

In its constant drive for innovation Roca presents In-Tank, a new revolution in bathroom spaces. It is a unique technology in the market, enabling the cistern to be incorporated into the WC. It is also notable for its design, water-saving capability and its quiet flush. In-Tank shows you what WCs of the future will be like.

Available in the Meridian Collection

Marazzi. Your space.

Timeless classical.
The new Treverkchic porcelain stoneware and
the ageless beauty of Calacatta marble-look slabs.

www.marazzi.it

PH. ANDREA FERRARI

MARAZZI

www.modulnova.it
MODULNOVA
KITCHEN LIVING BATH
milano london paris

DECOR WALTHER

BATHROOM ACCESSORIES LIGHTING MIRRORS

KITCHENPAPER*

*All you need to heat things up in the kitchen

'TIBU' STOOL, £780, BY ANDERSSEN & VOLL, FOR MAGIS. THREE-PART 'ETKØKKEN' KITCHEN (SINK, BLOCK WITH KNIFE, COOKING UNITS), PRICE ON REQUEST, BY METTE SCHELDE STUDIO. OIL AND VINEGAR SET, £245, BY BOTTEGA VENETA. TAJINE, €88; PAN, €54, BOTH BY KNINDUSTRIE. 'LAYER LONDON' DOOR, €582 PER SQ M, BY PIERO LISSONI, FOR LUALDI. 'PROP' LIGHT, €1,578, BY BERTJAN POT, FOR MOOOI

FOR STOCKISTS, SEE PAGE 054

Rossana Showroom Mayfair
London opening soon

DC10 / design Vincenzo De Cotiis
www.rossana.com / info@rossana.it

ROSSANA

⬇ 'SINE TEMPORE' KITCHEN SYSTEM
by Valcucine

Making use of inlays, carvings, mosaics and a high degree of customisation, this kitchen series amounts to a virtually bespoke service. At its heart is a section added to the worktop, available in a range of aluminium, stainless steel or stone finishes (pictured). This can contain, or conceal, everything from a herb garden to all the essential kitchen equipment. *'Sine Tempore' kitchen system, from £1,600 per m, by Valcucine, www.valcucine.com*

⬆ 'DF 461/460 VARIO' DISHWASHER
by Gaggenau

Gaggenau has stripped back its new dishwasher collection to the realm of pure function. Concealed from view behind unit fronts, and available in two heights with various hinging options, these fully integrated machines offer almost limitless positional possibilities, while a new speed programme completes in under an hour. *'DF 460/461 Vario' dishwasher, from €2,070, by Gaggenau, www.gaggenau.com*

⬆ 'XTEND+' SHELF UNIT
by Leicht

'Xtend+' is a wall-fitted aluminium shelving system with individually lit shelves, featuring remotely controlled horizontal slats that can be closed to form a smooth wall surface or opened entirely or partially, and individually, reimagining the space above the countertop. There's no need for a separate remote – the control app is available for your iPhone. *'Xtend+' shelf unit, from £3,000 per unit, by Leicht, www.leicht.com*

→ 'NUAGE' EXTRACTOR HOOD
by Fabrizio Crisà

Elica practically invented the extractor hood as high art. But its latest collection, by Fabrizio Crisà, couldn't be more self-effacing. 'Nuage' is designed expressly to blend into the kitchen architecture, and the external panel can be covered with plasterboard, tiles or paint. Beneath the hood, both filter and vented versions are available, while LED strips offer a natural, daytime lighting effect.
'Nuage' extractor hood, from £1,000,
by Fabrizio Crisà, for Elica, www.elica.com

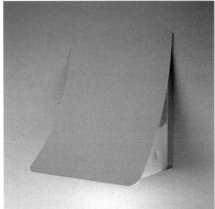

↑ 'P'7350' KITCHEN
by Poggenpohl and Porsche Design Studio

German brands Poggenpohl and Porsche Design Studio have joined forces to create the 'P'7340' kitchen. Porsche's subtle, masculine design aesthetic is clear to see. Kitchen elements can be slotted into an aluminium framework in any configuration, while the finishes – black-lacquer worktops, open-grained wood and anodised metallics – marry form and function. **Sujata Burman**
'P'7350' kitchen, price on request, by Poggenpohl
and Porsche Design Studio, www.poggenpohl.com

→ 'FLEXINDUCTION' HOB
by Bosch

We were, we will admit, slow to come around to the many virtues of the induction hob. Easy-to-clean functionality is all very well, but it hardly quickens the pulse. Real chefs, we thought, like real flame. We were, we will admit, wrong. A new range of induction hobs from German manufacturer Bosch, doesn't just look the part, but offers 17 different heat settings, reaches working temperature faster than can conceivably be possible and brings a pan of water to the boil in half the time of a conventional gas burner. The watchword here is flexibility. The clue is in the name.
'Flexinduction' hob, £1,299, by Bosch,
www.bosch-home.co.uk

PHOTOGRAPHY: ALBERTO ZANETTI ILLUSTRATOR: MAGDA ANTONIUK

Block rocking treats

The hottest kitchens at this year's EuroCucina fair in Milan included
a rock star, a diamond solitaire and a powdered-steel scene stealer

PHOTOGRAPHY: BEPPE BRANCATO INTERIORS: AMY HEFFERNAN

KITCHEN
ROCK

PRODUCER
STEININGER

DESIGNERS
MARTIN STEININGER
AND ALBERTO MINOTTI

CONTACT
WWW.STEININGER-
DESIGNERS.AT

FEATURES
AN HOMAGE TO ADOLF LOOS
AND DONALD JUDD, THE
KITCHEN'S FOUR MONOLITHIC
BLOCKS CAN BE GROUPED
TO FORM AN ISLAND OR
PRESENTED AS STANDALONE
CUBES. DESIGNED IN
COLLABORATION WITH
ALBERTO MINOTTI, OF MINOTTI
CUCINE, THE CUBES ARE MADE
OF 6MM-THICK, BEVELLED,
NATURAL STONE PANELS.

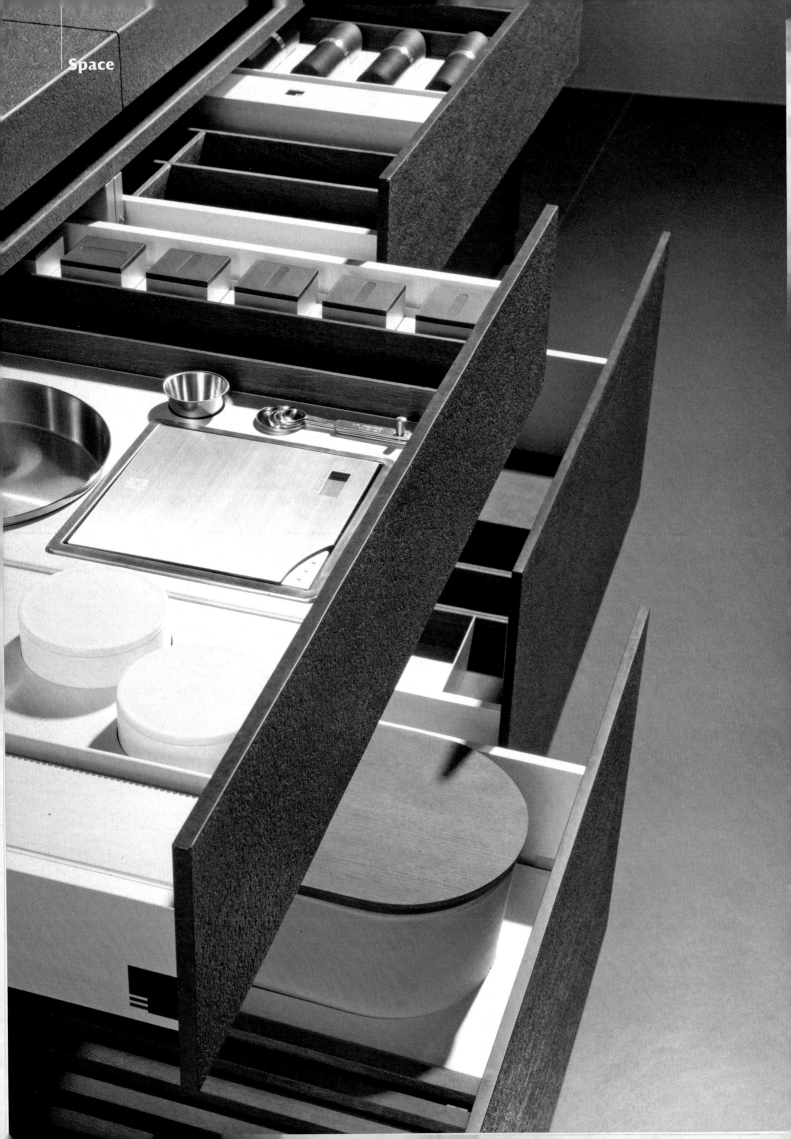

Chef's specials

The world's tastiest new kitchens are
wonderful workshops for culinary craftsmen

PHOTOGRAPHY: FRANK HÜLSBÖMER

EGGERSMANN

KITCHEN MODEL
TOKIO

MATERIALS
CONCRETE, VINTAGE OAK AND
HOT-ROLLED STAINLESS STEEL

ACCESSORIES, INCLUDING
SCALES AND BREAD BIN,
FROM EGGERSMANN'S 'BOXTEC'
RANGE, PART OF KITCHEN

CONTACT
WWW.EGGERSMANN.COM

KITCHEN MODEL
UNIQUE NERO ASSOLUTO

MATERIALS
NERO ASSOLUTO GRANITE
WITH WATERJET FINISH,
SMOKED EUCALYPTUS VENEER

OVEN, BY V-ZUG

PLAIN ENGLISH

OSEA KITCHEN, AS BEFORE,
FEATURING A CONCRETE SINK.
BOWL, £45; BRUSH, £35, BOTH
FROM TURNER & HARPER.
NAPKIN, £11.50, FROM FOLKLORE.
SCOURER, £4, FROM THE
CONRAN SHOP. WKH 120 WPS
WASHING MACHINE, £1,299,
BY MIELE, FROM JOHN LEWIS

PHOTOGRAPHY: TOBIAS HARVEY INTERIORS: AMY HEFFERNAN

SMALLBONE

KITCHEN MODEL
NEW BRASSERIE

DESIGNER
PETER SHEPPARD

MATERIALS
STAINLESS STEEL, OAK, GLASS

CONTACT
WWW.SMALLBONE.CO.UK

TEPPAN YAKI, £1,800; STEAM OVEN,
£1,275; OVEN, £1,700, ALL BY
GAGGENAU. 'TWIN207' KNIFE SKNIFE,
£369, BY MATTEO THUN, FOR
ZWILLING JA HENCKELS. COCOTTE,
£160, BY STAUB. GRATER WITH CHEESE
CELLAR, £55, BY KUNO PREY, FOR
ALESSI. 'GRILLIT', £85, BY LE CREUSET

SMALLBONE

NEW BRASSERIE KITCHEN, AS
BEFORE. 'ALL-TIME' WINE GLASSES;
TUMBLERS, £5.50 EACH, ALL BY
GUIDO VENTURINI, FOR ALESSI.
'BIG APPLE' DECANTER, £60,
BY RIEDEL CRYSTAL. BREAKFAST
CUP AND SAUCER SETS, £29 EACH;
DINNER PLATES, £22.50 EACH; JUG,
£44.50 ALL BY BRANKSOME CHINA.

'WEATHER DIARY' PLATES
(TOP RIGHT), £32 AND £24,
BY AINO-MAIJA METSOLA
AND SAMI RUOTSALAINEN,
FOR MARIMEKKO; GARLIC POT,
£35, BY TERAFEU TERAFOUR,
ALL FROM TWENTYTWENTYONE.
JADEITE TUMBLER, £13;
JUG £35, BOTH FROM LIBERTY

PHOTOGRAPHY: TOBIAS HARVEY INTERIORS: AMY HEFFERNAN

BETTELUX SILHOUETTE SIDE
Precise angular exterior with gently contoured interior.
Made from high-grade steel/enamel with a 30 year warranty.

Design: Tesseraux + Partner

www.bette.de

SIEMATIC

KITCHEN MODEL
INDIVIDUAL DESIGN CONCEPT,
ALLOWING THE COMBINING
OF CABINETS FROM DIFFERENT
KITCHENS TO CREATE
YOUR CUSTOM VERSION

MATERIALS
FROM LEFT, FULL-LENGTH
SE 4004 N CABINETS IN
NATURAL WALNUT FINISH;
SE 5005 L CABINETS IN
GRAPHITE GRAY GLOSS
FINISH; S2 WALL-HUNG,
LOW AND ISLAND CABINETS

CONTACT
WWW.SIEMATIC.CO.UK

PHOTOGRAPHY: FRANK HÜLSBÖMER

STONE SEDUCTIONS

Granite: Nero Assoluto Memorial Polished. Croco Design

Antolini presents Natura Collection.
The lightness of the design as a pure energy to
shape magical, unique expressions of creativity, strength
and versatility. Is there anything more changeable than stone?
antolini.com

Antolini®
ITALY

SIEMATIC

INDIVIDUAL DESIGN CONCEPT KITCHEN, AS BEFORE. DRAWERS FEATURE USB CHARGING POINT, ALUMINIUM DRAWER DIVIDERS AND SIEMATIC'S SPICE JARS. IPAD AIR, FROM £399, BY APPLE. CUTLERY, FROM A SELECTION, BY WMF

FOR STOCKISTS, SEE PAGE 054

Stockists

Block, part of the Solitaires kitchen, by **Bulthaup**. See page 033 of our Kitchens & Bathrooms supplement

A

Agape
Tel: 39.0376 250311 (Italy)
www.agapedesign.it

Agape12
Tel: 39.02 6556 0296 (Italy)
www.agape12.it

Alessi
Tel: 44.20 7518 9090 (UK)
www.alessi.com

Another Country
www.anothercountry.com

Antrax IT
Tel: 44.1342 302250 (UK)
www.antrax.it

Apple
www.apple.com

Aria
Tel: 44.20 7704 6222 (UK)
www.ariashop.co.uk

Armani/Roca
www.armaniroca.com

Astro Lighting
Tel: 44.1279 427001 (UK)
www.astrolighting.co.uk

B

Balineum
Tel: 44.20 7431 9364 (UK)
www.balineum.co.uk

Benchmark
Tel: 44.1488 608020 (UK)
www.benchmarkfurniture.com

Bio A+oE
Tel: 39.0522 303 246 (Italy)
www.bioaoe.com

Bisque
Tel: 44.1276 605888 (UK)
www.bisque.co.uk

Bottega Venetta
Tel: 44.800 157 7356 (UK)
www.bottegaveneta.com

Branksome China
Tel: 44.20 7351 2130 (UK)
www.branksomechina.co.uk

Brix
Tel: 39.02 8738 7900 (Italy)
www.brixweb.com

C

Ceramica Cielo
Tel: 39.0761 56701 (Italy)
www.ceramicacielo.com

Chanel
www.chanel.com

Christophe Robin
Tel: 33.1 40 20 92 12 (France)
www.christophe-robin.com

Christy
www.christy-towels.com

Compagnie de Provence
Tel: 33.4 95 06 30 20 (France)
www.compagniedeprovence.com

The Conran Shop
Tel: 44.844 848 4000 (UK)
www.conranshop.co.uk

Couto
www.couto.pt

CP Hart
Tel: 44.845 873 1121 (UK)
www.cphart.co.uk

D

Darkroom London
Tel: 44.20 7831 7244 (UK)
www.darkroomlondon.com

De'Longhi
www.delonghi.co.uk

Décor Walther
Tel: 49.69 272279 0 (Germany)
www.decor-walther.de

Designer Box
Tel: 33.6 72 91 87 85 (France)
www.designerbox.com

Diptyque
Tel: 44.800 840 0010 (UK)
www.diptyqueparis.co.uk

E

Earthborn Paints
Tel: 44.1928 734171 (UK)
www.earthbornpaints.co.uk

Ex.t
Tel: 39.055 3457 182 (Italy)
www.ex-t.com

F

Fantini
Tel: 39.0322 918411 (Italy)
www.fantini.it

Farrow & Ball
Tel: 44.1202 876141 (UK)
www.farrow-ball.com

Folklore
Tel: 44.20 7354 9333 (UK)
www.shopfolklore.com

G

Gaggenau
www.gaggenau.com

Geo F Trumper
Tel: 44.20 7272 1765 (UK)
www.trumpers.com

The Goodhood Store
Tel: 44.20 7729 3600 (UK)
goodhoodstore.com

Graff
www.graff-faucets.com

H

Harvey Maria
Tel: 44.845 680 1231 (UK)
www.harveymaria.com

I

Ila
Tel: 44.1608 677676 (UK)
www.ila-spa.com

Inbani
Tel: 34.965 106 465 (Spain)
www.inbani.com

J

John Lewis
Tel: 44.8456 049049 (UK)
www.johnlewis.com

JosephJoseph
www.josephjoseph.com

K

Kaldewei
Tel: 44.1480 498053 (UK)
www.kaldewei.com

KnIndustrie
www.knindustrie.com

Koh-I-Noor
www.koh-i-noor.it

L

Le Creuset
Tel: 44.800 373792 (UK)
www.lecreuset.co.uk

Liberty
Tel: 44.20 7734 1234 (UK)
www.liberty.co.uk

Lualdi
Tel: 39.02 978 9248 (Italy)
www.lualdiporte.com

M

MAC Cosmetics
Tel: 44.800 054 2999 (UK)
www.maccosmetics.com

Magis
Tel: 39.04 2131 9600 (Italy)
www.magisdesign.com

Makro
Tel: 39.049 99 10 951 (Italy)
www.makro.it

Marazzi
Tel: 39.059 384111 (Italy)
www.marazzi.it

Mercury
www.mercuryappliances.co.uk

Mette Schelde
Tel: 45.2688 8004 (Denmark)
www.metteschelde.com

Mikiya Kobayashi
Tel: 81.3 6421 3926 (Japan)
www.mikiyakobayashi.com

Modulnova
Tel: 39.0434 425425 (Italy)
www.modulnova.com

Moooi
Tel: 31.76 578 4444
(The Netherlands)
www.moooi.com

Muji
www.muji.eu

Mutina
Tel: 39.0536 812800 (Italy)
www.mutina.it

N

Net-a-Porter
Tel: 44.800 044 5700 (UK)
www.net-a-porter.com

Nomess
Tel: 45.39 209 209 (Denmark)
www.nomess.dk

P

Paola C
Tel: 39.02 862409 (Italy)
www.paolac.com

R

Renova
www.myrenova.com

Riedel Crystal
Tel: 44.844 800 1143 (UK)
riedel.com

S

Samuel Heath
Tel: 44.121 766 4200 (UK)
www.samuel-heath.com

SCP
Tel: 44.20 7739 1869 (UK)
www.scp.co.uk

Selfridges
Tel: 44.800 123400 (UK)
www.selfridges.com

Sfera
www.ricordi-sfera.com

Siematic
Tel: 44.161 246 6010 (UK)
www.siematic.com

Society
www.societylimonta.com

Space NK
Tel: 44.20 8740 2085 (UK)
spacenk.com

Spazio Rossana Orlandi
Tel: 39.02 467 4471 (Italy)
www.rossanaorlandi.com

Staub
www.staub.fr

Studio WM
Tel: 31.64 578 4065
(The Netherlands)
www.studiowm.com

T

Tubes Radiatori
www.tubesradiatori.com

Turner & Harper
www.turnerandharper.com

Twentytwentyone
Tel: 44.20 7288 1996 (UK)
www.twentytwentyone.com

V

Vano Alto
Tel: 33.61 657233 (Italy)
www.vanoalto.it

Vitra
www.vitra.com

Vola
Tel: 44.1525 72 01 11 (UK)
www.vola.com

V-Zug
www.vzug.com

W

WMF
www.wmf.com

Z

Zucchetti
Tel: 44.845 600 0400 (UK)
www.zucchettidesign.it

Zucchetti Kos
Tel: 39.0322 954700 (Italy)
www.zucchettikos.com

Zwilling JA Henckels
Tel: 44.845 262 1731 (UK)
www.zwilling.com

SAMUEL HEATH
since 1820

STYLE
MODERNE

Purism. Sensuality. Intelligence.
To see what else bulthaup kitchens have to offer, please
contact your local retail partner www.bulthaup.com

bulthaup

Aviator chic for frequent-flying Amelia Earharts–p204 Killer cuts at the Paris couture shows A happy afterlife for design dead stock–p214 London's L'Anima café offering all-day delights and Claudio Silvestrin interiors Philippe Parreno's stuffed spleen–p226 Saskia de Brauw mixing media at the Edinburgh International Fashion Festival

This page, coat, £4,000;
jacket, £2,350; knitted
collar, £270; trousers, £760,
all by **Dior**. Top, £425, by
Pringle of Scotland.
Shoes, £410, by **Adieu**

Opposite, coat, £2,080;
sunglasses, £450, both by
Louis Vuitton. Jumper,
€650, by **Nina Ricci**.
Trousers, £235, by **Joseph**

Ground control

Aviator glamour takes the pre-fall collections to new heights

Photography Rory Payne *Fashion* Verity Parker

This page, coat, £1,460,
by **Jean Paul Gaultier**.
Knitted collar, £270, by **Dior**.
Jumper, £60, by **Uniqlo**

Opposite, coat, £1,300,
by **Boss**. Fur jacket, price
on request, by **Philipp Plein**.
Jumper, £290, by **Jean Paul
Gaultier**. Trousers, £600,
by **Marni**. Shoes, £620,
by **Saint Laurent by Hedi
Slimane**. Goggles, from
Contemporary Wardrobe

This page, cape, £600;
jacket, £1,700; skirt, £250,
all by **Acne Studios**.
Shirt, £290, by **Vanessa
Bruno**. Goggles, from
Contemporary Wardrobe

Opposite, cape, £1,145, by
**Saint Laurent by Hedi
Slimane**. Dress, £484,
by **JW Anderson**. Jumper,
£490, by **Vanessa Bruno**

This page, jacket, £3,000,
by **Christopher Kane**.
Top, £605; shirt, £865;
skirt, £500, all by **Prada**.
Belt, price on request,
by **Proenza Schouler**.
Boots, £1,120, by **Louis
Vuitton**. Goggles, from
Contemporary Wardrobe

Opposite, jacket, £3,280,
by **Chanel**. Boiler suit,
from **Contemporary
Wardrobe**. Brooch, £215,
by **Jean Paul Gaultier**

Fashion

This page, coat, £2,055,
by **Bottega Veneta**. Jumper,
£350, by **Saint Laurent
by Hedi Slimane**. Skirt, £750,
by **Michael Kors**. Boots, price
on request, by **Fendi**. Gloves,
£170, by **Jean Paul Gaultier**

Opposite, fur jacket, £3,290,
by **Gucci**. Pinstripe jacket,
£1,678; trousers, £815, both
by **Alexander McQueen**.
Jumper, £100, by **Acne Studios**.
Boots, £410, by **Adieu**. Hat,
from **Contemporary Wardrobe**

For stockists, see page 224

Model: Emma Champtaloup
at Viva London

Hair: Nao Kawakami
using Moroccanoil

Make-up: Jenny Coombs
at Streeters using
Bobbi Brown Cosmetics

Casting: Julia Lange

Photographer's assistants:
Matthew Healy,
Willow Williams

Fashion assistant: Sarah Starkey

Digital operator: Dave Imms

TAKING STOCK

The furniture factory's shut down, but we're loath to move out

Photography Leandro Farina *Interiors* Hana Al-Sayed

'Inchino' lamp, £880, by
Antonino Sciortino, for
Busnelli, from **Chaplins**.
'PK80' daybed, £12,901,
by **Poul Kjærholm**, for
Fritz Hansen. Plant stand,
£32, by **Ferm Living**;
plant pot, £19, by **Hay**, both
from **The Goodhood Store**.
'Cuoio Lounge Grand'
armchair, £1,684, by **Walter
Knoll**, from **Aram Store**.
'Bidjar Highgate Enjoy'
carpet, from the Erased
Heritage collection, £2,155
per sq m, by **Jan Kath**.
'835 Infinito' shelves, from
£5,500, by **Franco Albini**,
for **Cassina**. Decanter, £450,
by **Joe Cariati Glass**, from
The Conran Shop. Balsabox
Personal box, €119, by
Nomess Copenhagen.
Small candleholder, £15; large,
£26, both by **Eno Studio**,
from **Nook**. 'Grid' vase,
€330, by **Jaime Hayon**, for
Gaia & Gino. 'Kyo' chairs,
£1,310 each, by **Walter Knoll**,
from **Aram Store**. 'Bean'
desk, £22,828, by **Roberto
Lazzeroni**, for **Ceccotti
Collezioni**, from **Mayfair
Design Studio**. Madison
pen, £160, by **Caran
d'Ache**. Pencil case, £75,
from **Choosing Keeping**.
'Coil' lamp, $495, by **Castor**.
'ID' chair, £1,213, by
Antonio Citterio, for **Vitra**.
'Clouded Slate' paint, £24 per
2.5 litres, by **Dulux**

Space

'Dania' stepladder, £239, by **Skagerak**, from **Twentytwentyone**. 'One Step Up' shelving unit, £276, by **Francis Cayouette**, for **Normann Copenhagen**, from **Aria**. 'Rosettenhenkel' vases, €3,454 each, by **Karl Friedrich Schinkel**, for **KPM**. 1930s sharpening machine, £145, from **Choosing Keeping**. Akita tape dispenser, £120, by **Tatsuya Akita**, for **Plant & Moss**. Big Spanish brush, £12, from **Present & Correct**. BuzziBoxes, £99 each, by **BuzziSpace**. 'Silence' carpet, £69 per sq m, by **Bolon**. 'LC14' stools, from £462, by **Le Corbusier**, for **Cassina**. Atomic lighting tubes, €823 each, by **Małgorzata Ratajczak and Sebastian Szlabs**, for **Emandes**. '45° Vetrina' display case, £4,024, by **Ron Gilad**, for **Molteni & C.** 'Mocha' pot, €296, by **Marguerite Friedlaender**, for **KPM**. Candleholders, €200 each, by **KPM**. 'Steelwood Galvanised' chair, £418, by **Ronan & Erwan Bouroullec**, for **Magis**, from **Twentytwentyone**. 'Confair' tables, price on request, by **Andreas Störiko**, for **Wilkhahn**. Towel Ladder, €402, by **Norm Architects**, for **Menu**. 'Copenhague' chairs, £247 each, by **Ronan & Erwan Bouroullec**, for **Hay**. Brass clip, £6, by **Hay**; forms, £1 each, both from **Present & Correct**. Taxus pen, £79, by **Gerd A Müller**, for **Lamy**. String, £7, from **Labour and Wait**. 'Lunar Falls' paint (upper wall); 'Bleached Lichen 3' (lower wall), £24 per 2.5 litres, both by **Dulux**

Space

'Concorde' dining table,
£3,361, by **Emmanuel Gallina**,
for **Poliform**. 'Crystal Rock'
lights, from £680, by **Arik Levy**,
for **Lasvit**. On table, from left,
Enamoramento sculpture,
€248, by **Cristina Leiria**,
for **Vista Alegre**. 'Pebble' vase,
£1,550, by **Kate Hume**, for
When Objects Work, from
The Conran Shop. 'Fusion'
rechargeable lamp, price on
request, by **Noé Duchaufour-
Lawrance**, for **Gaia & Gino**.
Disquiet Luxurians (set of
chisels and ram), £1,500,
by **Emilie F Grenier**. 'Double
Herkimer' vase, from the Giants
Collection, price on request,
by **Arik Levy**, for **Gaia & Gino**.
Exótica crystal box, €350,
by **Vista Alegre**. 'Filigree Spirit
Fruit with coloured canes'
glass centrepiece, £5,900,
by **Jeremy Maxwell Wintrebert**,
from **Vessel Gallery**. 'Boa' vase,
£2,990, by **Lalique**. 'Gravity'
vase, £435, by **Vanessa Mitrani**,
from **FBC London**. 'Dent' chair,
£354, by **O4i**, for **Blå Station**.
'Azure Fusion 1' paint,
£24 per 2.5 litres, by **Dulux**

Clockwise from front centre, 'Allout' table, £730, by **Go Modern**. 'Series 3300' easy chair, £3,528, by **Arne Jacobsen**, for **Fritz Hansen**. 'Zero' fabric, £46 per m, by **Nya Nordiska**. 'Reel' side table, £2,391, by **Atelier Oï**, for **B&B Italia**. Carry On wheelbarrow, €494, by **Francesco Faccin**, for **Officinanove**, from **All About Design**. 'Moulds' lamp, €1,150, by **Jan Plechac & Henry Wielgus**, for **Lasvit**. 'Tizio' lamp, £430, by **Richard Sapper**, for **Artemide**. Chair, £1,420 for two, by **Reed and Delphine Krakoff**, for **Established & Sons**. 'Sedia' chair, €265, by **Enzo Mari**, for **Artek**. BuzziCube 3D seats, £410 each, by **BuzziSpace**. 'This Way' mirror, €199, by **Thomas Schnur**, for **Details, Produkte + Ideen**. 'Algue', £55 per box, by **Ronan & Erwan Bouroullec**, for **Vitra**. 'Residential' sofa, £3,324, by **Architecture & Associés**, for **Knoll**. 'Smokey Slate' paint, £24 per 2.5 litres, by **Dulux**

'Schraag' table, £1,700, by **Maarten van Severen**, from **Bulo**. 'Finnieston' lamp, £445, by **Samuel Chan**, for **Channels**. No.1 & No.2 Screwdriver Set, £40, by **Elemen'tary**, from **Nook**. Hammer, £48, from **Labour and Wait**. Try squares, 6in, £12; 9in, £16, both by **Joseph Marples**, from **Objects of Use**. 'Weight Here' candleholder, €54, by **KiBiSi**; 'Afteroom' chairs, €200 each, by **Afteroom**, both for **Menu**. 'Flux!' sideboard, price on request, by **Patrick Schols**. 'Toio' lamp, £761, by **Achille Castiglioni**, for **Flos**. 'Albero' shelves, £7,840, by **Gianfranco Frattini**, for **Poltrona Frau**. Watering can, £36, by **Haws**, from **Nook**. 'Charred Commodes', $1,250 each, by **Michael Moran and Celia Gibson**, for **Moran Woodworked**

Furniture. 'Low Black Poly Cabinet', price on request, by **Max Lamb**, courtesy of **Gallery Fumi**. 'Ausgebrannt' burnt-log stool, €900, by **Kaspar Hamacher**. 'Urushi' stool (just seen), price on request, by **Max Lamb**, courtesy of **Gallery Fumi**. 'Bench Mould Shelves' (just seen, against wall), from £900 per shelf, by **Glithero**. Rug, €14,450, by **Helmut Lang**, for **Henzel Studio**. 'Frayed Hessian 1' paint, £24 per 2.5 litres, by **Dulux**

For stockists, see page 224

Photographer's assistants:
Gabby Laurent, Nathan Perkins

Interiors assistants:
Camille Boyer, Thomas Durrant, Tamzen Grove, Darcey Williamson, Jennifer Crouch

Stockists

A

Acne Studios
Tel: 44.20 7589 5995 (UK)
www.acnestudios.com

Adieu at Net-a-Porter
www.netaporter.com

Afteroom
Tel: 46.761 699 891 (Sweden)
afteroom.com

Alexander McQueen
Tel: 44.20 7355 0088 (UK)
www.alexandermcqueen.com

All About Design
Tel: 44.20 3119 1111 (UK)
www.puntoit.co.uk

Aram Store
Tel: 44.20 7557 7557 (UK)
www.aram.co.uk

Aria
Tel: 44.20 7704 6222 (UK)
www.ariashop.co.uk

Artek
Tel: 358.10 617 3480 (Finland)
www.artek.fi

Artemide
Tel: 39.02 935181 (Italy)
www.artemide.com

Atelier Polyhedre
Tel: 33.6 82 24 79 50 (France)
www.polyhedre.com

B

B&B Italia
Tel: 39.031 795 111 (Italy)
www.bebitalia.com

Baxter
Tel: 39.03 135999 (Italy)
www.baxter.it

Bolon
Tel: 46.321 53 04 00 (Sweden)
www.bolon.com

Bosa
Tel: 39.0423 561483 (Italy)
www.bosatrade.com

Boss
Tel: 44.20 7554 5700 (UK)
www.hugoboss.com

Bottega Veneta
Tel: 44.20 7838 9394 (UK)
www.bottegaveneta.com

Brix
Tel: 39.02 87387900 (Italy)
www.brixweb.com

Bulo
Tel: 44.20 7253 0055 (UK)
www.bulo.com

BuzziSpace
Tel: 44.20 7253 3363 (UK)
www.buzzispace.com

C

Calvin Klein
Tel: 44.20 3100 2900 (UK)
www.calvinklein.com

Cappellini
www.cappellini.it

Caran d'Ache
www.carandache.com

Carven at Oki-Ni
oki-ni.com

Cassina
Tel: 44.20 7584 0000 (UK)
www.cassina.com

Castor
Tel: 1.416 994 1232 (Canada)
www.castordesign.ca

CC-Tapis
Tel: 39.02 8909 3884 (Italy)
www.cc-tapis.com

Chanel
Tel: 44.20 7493 5040 (UK)
www.chanel.com

Channels
Tel: 44.20 7371 0301 (UK)
www.channelsdesign.com

Chaplins
Tel: 44.20 7352 6195 (UK)
www.chaplins.co.uk

Choosing Keeping
Tel: 44.20 7613 3842 (UK)
choosingkeeping.com

**Christopher Kane
at Dover Street Market**
Tel: 44.20 7518 0680 (UK)
www.doverstreetmarket.com

The Conran Shop
Tel: 44.20 7723 2223 (UK)
www.conranshop.co.uk

Contemporary Wardrobe
Tel: 44.20 7713 7370 (UK)
www.contemporarywardrobe.com

D

Dante Goods and Bads
www.dante.lu

De Castelli
Tel: 39.0423 638218 (Italy)
www.decastelli.com

Desalto
Tel: 39.031 783 2211 (Italy)
www.desalto.it

Details, Produkte + Ideen
Tel: 49.221 9 32 09 10 (Germany)
www.details-produkte.de

Dior Homme at Harrods
Tel: 44.20 7730 1234 (UK)
www.dior.com

Dior
Tel: 44.20 7172 0172 (UK)
www.dior.com

Domus
Tel: 44.20 7458 4000 (UK)
www.domustiles.com

Dossofiorito
Tel: 39.34 06235800 (Italy)
www.dossofiorito.com

Dulux
Tel: 44.8444 817817 (UK)
www.dulux.com

E

Emandes
Tel: 48.604 61 33 32 (Poland)
www.emandes.com

Emilie F Grenier
www.commedesmachines.com

Emporio Armani
Tel: 44.20 7823 8818 (UK)
www.armani.com

Established & Sons
Tel: 44.20 7608 0990 (UK)
www.establishedandsons.com

Exteta
Tel: 39.0362 308095 (Italy)
www.exteta.it

F

Fabriano
www.fabrianoboutique.com

Cape, £2,625; jumper, £750,
both by **Chloé**. Trousers,
£1,660, by **Proenza
Schouler**. See page 204

FBC London
Tel: 44.20 7730 9555 (UK)
www.fbc-london.com

Fendi
Tel: 44.20 7838 6288 (UK)
www.fendi.com

Flexform
Tel: 39.03 62 3991 (Italy)
www.flexform.it

Flos
Tel: 39.0302438 1 (Italy)
www.flos.com

Fritz Hansen
Tel: 44.20 7637 5534 (UK)
www.fritzhansen.com

G

Gaia & Gino
Tel: 420.222 315 739
(Czech Republic)
www.gaiagino.com

Gallery Fumi
Tel: 44.20 7490 2366 (UK)
www.galleryfumi.com

Giorgetti
Tel: 39.03 6275275 (Italy)
www.giorgetti-spa.com

Glas Italia
Tel: 39.03 9232 3202 (Italy)
www.glasitalia.com

Glithero
Tel: 44.20 7272 3629 (UK)
www.glithero.com

Go Modern
Tel: 44.20 7731 9540 (UK)
www.gomodern.co.uk

The Goodhood Store
Tel: 44.20 7729 3600 (UK)
www.goodhoodstore.com

Gucci
Tel: 44.20 7629 2716 (UK)
www.gucci.com

H

Hay
Tel: 44.7703 676020 (UK)
hay.dk

Hayon
Tel: 34.93 630 7772 (Spain)
www.hayonstudio.com

Henzel Studio
Tel: 46.7 6339 9900 (Sweden)
www.byhenzel.com

J

Jan Kath
Tel: 49.221 94967 940 (Germany)
www.jan-kath.de

**Jean Paul Gaultier
at Layers London**
Tel: 44.20 7495 1296 (UK)
www.layerslondon.com

Joseph
www.joseph-fashion.com

K

Kaspar Hamacher
Tel: 32.47 06 11 79 6 (Belgium)
www.kasparhamacher.be

Correction
W*183, Hot ticket, page 061.
The Curzon Victoria is housed in 62 Buckingham Gate by Pelli Clarke Pelli Architects, delivered by Swanke Hayden Connell Architects.

NEXT MONTH

The Handmade Issue 2014

For our fifth annual celebration of craft and design, we've commissioned some of the world's finest makers, artists and manufacturers to create one-off wonders especially for you. If you didn't catch them at our show in Salone del Mobile, here's a taste of what's to come...

Vincenzo De Cotiis turns the table on a wondrous set of Jaguar wheels

----

The Ace Hotel's Lovage serves up life-enhancing elixirs

Bally lets loose with hell-for-leather skis

Todd Bracher pops a corking jacket

Jeff Zimmerman and **Michael Reynolds** tease with hand-blown glass sex toys

----

Plus, punchy boxing gloves, a simply cracking croquet set, glow-in-the-dark wallpaper, a perfectly packed lunch box and lots more

----

ON SALE 10 JULY

PHILIPPE PARRENO'S
Stuffed spleen

French multimedia artist Philippe Parreno (W*176) orchestrates his exhibitions (such as last year's critical smash at the Palais de Tokyo in Paris) like an immersive performance of film, objects and sound. The dish he has sent us is a harder sell. 'It is made from veal spleen stuffed with pork, veal fat, stale breadcrumbs, cumin, garlic, cayenne pepper, salt, pepper and parsley. Sounds disgusting but it's fantastic,' he maintains. 'The recipe comes from a book, a collection of Jewish-Spanish North African recipes, that was made for me by my late mother. These are very old recipes - you wouldn't find them in modern cookbooks, as people just don't eat like this anymore. My mother included sayings from her grandmother on the pages facing each recipe. It's morbid. My mother is dead, my great-grandmother is dead and the recipes are not cooked anymore. A book of death!' Still, don't let us put you off.
For Parreno's stuffed spleen recipe, visit Wallpaper.com or download the iPad edition at Wallpaper.com/iPad ✳

'Albi' silver-plated underplate, £388, by Christofle, from Harrods, www.harrods.com

PHOTOGRAPHY: JOHN SHORT INTERIORS: MARIA SOBRINO FOOD: MAUD EDEN WRITER: PAUL MCCANN